MOM PRENEUR

RUNNING A FAMILY
WHILE BEING A BOSS

TANISHA JAMISON

CONTENTS

It started with, what a man can do, a woman can try, then it turned to, what a man can do, a woman can do as well. At a particular time, it was, what a man can do a woman can do better. Now the real thing is, "what a man can do, a woman can overdo...".And this is very correct!

WHO AM I

I'm a mom of four kids. Jonas 1, Jameson 3, Roberto 17, all boys and Skyler, 11, who is my only girl. Roberto was born when I was only 16years old, though I struggled but I was able to finish my high school and college with the help of my mom keeping him all the time.

I and his father separated because of age and maturity. Then I had Skyler when I was in my early 20's. Still doing three jobs, because I'm a workaholic, I had to balance, combine my work and still fulfill my responsibility as a mom. I had to work a lot because the Dad couldn't keep a job! We eventually broke up when she was 2 years old.

Then I began to work as a nanny for some years until I decided to open a childcare center. That was my turning point! Within the first 2 years and with the help of my biological mother my capacity exploded.

In 2015, I met my present husband and we got legally married in 2018.

I and Donelle have a great and exciting relationship. My mother Lisa and his mom Sandra get along well. They help a lot with our two kids Jameson and Jonas. My two brothers and his sister have been of great help!

I am a successful entrepreneur. I work for many hours daily. I'm a busy mother. I make all the money. Even when I'm not out of the house I am occupied: doing my emails, researching, and learning about new ways to make more money.

My husband makes money but not nearly as much as I and that hurts him. We don't argue much but we argue a lot about allowing him to do more.

I tell him to be a stay at home dad but he doesn't feel like a man should do that.

But for now I am at the top of my game. I work and I think every woman should work. Even if your hubby is not a stay at home dad, there are lots of ways to cope!

As a mompreneur, how do I cope? How do I take care of my hubby and my kids? How do I run the house and run my business? How do I, cook, clean, take care of the kid's needs, and be a happy wife as well as a successful business person?

This book is your hand, is my attempt to answer the above questions and inspire you in your journey as a mompreneur. If I can do it, I believe you can do it too!

WHAT YOU NEED

The first thing you need is to understand your own personal attributes and identify the basic traits of a successful entrepreneur that you must necessarily acquire.

Optimism- For an entrepreneur, being able to think confidently and optimistically is a must. This desire to stay confident will get you through the tough spots you are eventually going to face.

Capacity to Initiate: Are you a visionary? Can you translate your vision to mission by initiating actions?

Leadership Ability -Do you like being in charge and bearing responsibility?

Resilience: Will you somehow pick up and move on when things go wrong or not exactly as you planned? Can you bounce back from failure without feeling any lasting pain?

Ability to listen-It is definitely necessary for a mompreneur to be able to communicate and "sell herself," but the ability to listen is very essential.

Ethics- Do you believe in acting with respect, justice, honesty and truthfulness with individuals? If you want to develop some kind of market, being viewed as truthful, transparent and trustworthy is crucial.

Ability to see the big picture: A good entrepreneur or business leader has to be able to view a dilemma from a variety of different angles and still come up with new solutions. You must be able to see, pursue and take others along toward the big picture you have seen

The potential to 'Spot a Trend': A successful business owner must be able to quickly spot a profitable trend they can capitalize on.

Not all who wishes to start working for themselves or venture into the capital market will have all of these 'characteristics,' but the good news is that if you are able to focus on what you want all these traits can be acquired.

The most important thing I think you need to become a good entrepreneur is the desire and motivation to learn. And that is the purpose behind this book

You will do well therefore if you key into all I have written in this book: chew, digest and apply them appropriately, so you can enter into a successful tomorrow as a mompreneur.

It goes without saying that becoming a mompreneur is better when the children are older and more autonomous.

The benefit of being pragmatic is that it allows you to be more centered when you know that you don't have endless hours to work on your company because of family and other responsibilities.

And imagine what happens when you're more focused on it?

You're getting more active (that's why you're concentrating on the right things of course).

Way too many moms are going to buy into the lie that they can have it all (or do it all and feel depressed or unhappy when they figure out they can't. The first change of mind that you ought to implement if you wish to excel is to be honest about your circumstances.

Be honest about how much time you can spend in your company, and then find out how to make the best of the time you have available.

START TREATING YOUR BUSINESS LIKE A REAL BUSINESS NOT A HOBBY

Do you handle your company as a serious business or a hobby? To thrive as a mompreneur or small business owner, you need to cultivate an entrepreneurial mentality.

What does it entail to have an entrepreneurial attitude?

Having an entrepreneurial mentality clearly implies that you recognize and acknowledge that you are accountable for the success and loss of your company. When you have an entrepreneurial mentality, you know that the decisions you take are either going to make or ruin your business.

ESSENTIAL MINDSET FOR STARTING MOMPRENEURS

A lot of mompreneurs are failing as a result of their mentality. If you're one of them, it's time to make some adjustments to your thinking so that you can make some significant progress in your business.

Trying to learn and build the right way of thinking is time-consuming and not always straightforward. But if you remain dedicated you can begin to see a change in your business.

BE HONEST ON HOW LONG YOU HAVE TO WORK

It's hard to make a lot of changes if you're continually exhausted or stressed because you don't have sufficient time to do what you need to do.. You need to be positive about the condition instead of getting depressed or sad about all the things you can't do.

The fact is how much time you have to focus on your enterprise depends on factors like the amount of children you have at home, their age, and how much support you have.

All too many of us are running our companies as hobbies. We've made very little effort yet to demand great things from our company.

This isn't how it operates.

And how do you handle your business as a serious enterprise, not a hobby? Here are several ways to do this:

Be compliant with that. Which means you're working on your company, whether you feel like it or not. You wake up every day or most days) and you get to work. One factor that tends to remain reliable is to have "regular business hours. That implies choosing the best time (for you to work on your business.)

Think regarding the qualities you need to excel. If you start taking your company seriously, you quit winging things and start knowing what you can about entrepreneurship and how to make your business work.

Reflect on and remove distractions. As you start treating your company seriously, you start to concentrate on things with the best return on investment. In other terms, you're removing distractions, because you're just paying attention to items that pass the needle. This means no longer having to compose a blog post when browsing across Facebook at the same time.

Become financially healthy. Understand the finances of your establishment, gains and losses. Know how to maximize your profits and get acquainted with Taxation and other financial facets of a business.

Be structured and provide a designated place that you use as a workplace.

When you start treating your business set up more than just a sport, your mood shifts and your concentration changes.

Cultivating entrepreneurial mentality is one of the greatest things you can do to help yourself in your business.

FORGET THE "DIY" MENTALITY

Let me just mention first of all that there's nothing wrong with wanting to do certain stuff. I'm doing a ton of things just to save money or because I have no budget for it. That's just how it is when you're an entrepreneur with little money to invest in your business. However as much as you can, you must be ready to put money into your business.

There are some things you don't need to waste your time and energy on. Don't attempt to "Google" everything all because you are versatile. As a growing entrepreneur, your time is very important. Therefore instead of doing some things personally you can just go ahead and outsource it while you are using your time to think and improve on your business,

DEVELOP A CONFIDENT MINDSET

Are you a confident business woman, or is self-doubt your major challenge? If you are continually doubting yourself or questioning if your goods or services are good enough you might be struggling with self-doubt. In fact might be dealing with a lack of self-confidence especially if you are always asking for opinions of people before making your decisions.

Shortage of confidence would deter you from achieving your goals. You keep selling yourself short because you lack confidence, and you believe what you have to give is not nearly as nice as what your competitor provides.

While it's essential to give value to your consumers or clients, and it's good practice to reach above and beyond. It can only remain a good practice as long as you get something equal and useful in exchange. Don't throw away all your profit because you believe that's the only way you can draw clients or customers. Be positive in what you're selling as long as you are offering something valuable, and beneficial.

If you're grappling with feelings of fear and self-doubt, here are several ways you can strengthen your confidence.

Surround yourself with others that are optimistic. Surround yourself with the good and the people who confirm and encourage you. Avoid contrasting yourself to the others. Do the best job you can and believe it's nice enough for you. Focus on your assets, not your weakness

Keep on learning. Don't really quit knowing. That's the best way to get stronger and strengthen your confidence. When you know "your things" there's no need to feel unsafe.

STOP BEING AFRAID OF THE COMPETITION

Do you waste much of your time staring over the fence into your competitor's world and trying to unnecessarily get concerned? Are you trying to stop yourself from doing things because you are afraid that others will steal your ideas? Believe it or not, this does happen. I know that certain entrepreneurs are reluctant to bring out their goods or services because they are afraid that their competitors will steal their concepts. The truth is that it is possible, especially if you are working in an online environment. But this should not to stop you from manifesting your creativity. At some point, you really have to stop thinking about what other individuals and businesses are doing and go ahead to do what you need to do. Excessive consideration of the competition will not benefit you. Once there are enough customers to go round, you just need to focus.

DON'T BE SACRED OF SUCCESSFUL ACHIEVEMENTS

In all honesty, I never used to think it was a possibility, but it is. Most mompreneurs are scared of achievement, even though they won't accept it. Some of them are frightened because they don't think they merit it they're terrified of transition, or for some other strange excuse. There are different ways in which the fear of performance expresses itself. The most popular approaches are to make life as complicated as possible for yourself and to undermine yourself. If you catch yourself making odd choices (or declining to make decisions that might make your business expand), or doing things that might actually hurt your businesses, you may want to question why you're scared of success or anything else. If you have a fear of performance, ask yourself why. What are you terrified of?

POSITIVE IMPACTS OF MOMPRENEURS

Kudos to women who ventured into the economic world with such enthusiastic drive as to generate spongy jealousy from their male counterpart .In the olden days, we used to describe motherhood as a lifetime mission of caring for kids and performing household duties alone. That has changed since! Women now play a critical function in adding to the economy, thereby demonstrating that they can also succeed in the labor market and become reputable entrepreneurs. So what are the benefits of "mompreneur-ship?"

WORKING MOMS ARE LESS PRONE TO DEPRESSION

Statistics suggest that a stay-at-home mom is more likely to have depression, which will take its toll on her children in turn. Children will only truly profit from seeing a disappointed mother around them who is stressed.

WORKING MOMS RAISE MORE INDEPENDENT KIDS

Working mothers' children tend to become more independent. As working moms need to teach children how to do chores on their own, at an early age, they develop a strong sense of responsibility.

KIDS CAN EASY LEARN THE VALUE OF MONEY AND DIGNITY OF LABOR

Because of double incomes, children belonging to households where both parents work have access to more jobs and better services. You may think this will make them spend money, but this is largely based on parenting. This is impossible to happen if parents instill in their kids the best beliefs. These kids are already watching their parents work hard to make a living.

In addition, they learn to realize where the money comes from and the value of budgeting and planning as they understand that their mother is struggling to contribute financially to the family.

Seeing their working mother handle time judiciously, along with the importance of money, often helps them value time. They learn how to prioritize and pick up useful expertise in time management.

WORKING MOMS ARE BETTER AT IGNORING THE "PARENTING POLICE"

Each parent is worried with how much time and attention their children should be provided. Working mothers, who are often thinly veiled as well-meaning friends, are often subject to constant pressure from the' parental police.' Not to mention all of the parental experts who have infiltrated the mainstream. Everybody is a specialist in parenting, it seems these days. The sensitive working mother realizes what the trade-offs are. She is confident enough to juggle her ability to pursue a career with the demands of parenting.

WORKING MOMS CAN BETTER MANAGE QUALITY TIME WITH THEIR KIDS

Everybody speaks with children about consistency or prime time. It is a sad fact that when they are with their kids, often parents are just half listening, since the other half is stuck to their computer. Working moms know that the minute they get home, they need to turn off and that they need to devote 100% of their valuable time to their children. E-mail, calls, and Facebook should all wait until the children are in bed. Working moms spend quality hours with their children to cover for the lack of time they don't spend together. Kids are still looking forward to their parents spending time with them. They should not take for granted the attention of their mother. A stay-at-home mom's children can get used to the attention of their mom around the clock and refuse to appreciate her efforts.

WORKING MOTHER'S KIDS ARE SMART

Compared to the children of non-working mothers, the kids of working mothers become smart and active. This is when all domestic tasks are left intact by the fact that the mothers have to step out of the home. The children behind understand their roles and manage to fulfill all their duties without

CHILDREN INCULCATE GOOD HABITS EASILY

Since returning from work, working mothers are now aided by their husband in household chores. Children learn good habits and inculcate ways of serving others as well as their mothers by watching the fathers being a helping hand to mothers, thereby inculcating in them good habits.

MOTHERS SHOWER MORE LOVE

Moms who work will be away from home and their children for long hours and will not spend much time with them. The implication of this is: whenever they show up, the likelihood of showering more love and affection is high. Though they spend little time, that little time inadvertently becomes quality time!

KIDS GET ADEQUATE FACILITIES

The woman, as she works, will be able to support her spouse in caseof money problems. This also assists to provide their children standard services, when they are not in any way short of money. The children are also allowed to attend extra classes and other events that wouldn't have been possible without enough cash

MOTHERS BECOME SOURCE OF INSPIRATION

Working moms are an inspiration to their kids as they look up to her and say they hope to be like their moms in the near future.

Working moms not only work, they also take care of their children without any trouble. So these kids don't need to look at anyone for inspiration, but they just get to see inspiration at home daily.

LIFE IS MORE THRILLING

Non-working moms are outgoing, rather they stay at home. They are not required to use or broaden their group of friend, but working moms are able to do so and send their kids out on outing anytime they feel. In this way kids often learn to socialize, communicate, and behave in front of others, while the mom is free from boredom

NO DEPENDENCE ON THE HUSBAND

There is no reason for a working mother to depend on her husband for income or anything . Without depending upon a husband, she becomes independent and receives her own pay. Without being indebted to anyone in the house, she is able to satisfy both her wishes and desires.

WORKING MOMS' KIDS HAVE FEWER BEHAVIORAL PROBLEMS

Many women fear that not having enough time with their children will translate to behavioral challenges. Upon looking at research findings from 1960, the reality is that working moms' children are not struggling at all. In certain instances, they have turned out to be well behaved than the mothers' children at home.

EMOTIONAL DEVELOPMENT OF THE KIDS IS NOT NEGATIVELY IMPACTED

A lot of study has been conducted at University College London to see if working mothers' children are going to grow up emotionally impoverished. The positive thing is that this is not the case at all. The secret is to have the right balance between work and parenting obligations. Daycare and a loving spouse, along with a mother-friendly business policy, make it completely possible.

WORKING MOMS TEND TO BE IN HAPPIER RELATIONSHIPS

Though much will depend on the spouse's mentality and support for the working mother, generally relationship of working moms tends to be happier than normal. I remember my father being very supportive of my mother, and he often took on the role of a supervisor to ensure that household chores were carried out. Many working mothers have found it easier to keep their relationship healthier, because they are happier and more satisfied. This could help to strengthen the relationship.

WORKING MOMS GET A BREAK

Though this may sound funny, its to the advantage of the working mom than she would not be under the excessive pressure of seeing all the household chores done!

The kids are flexible and resilient: Children of working moms understand that they need to be versatile and adapt to changing conditions. For example, they may get picked up from school a little later as mom is delayed at work. Or as Mom had to rush to the office for an early meeting, they might have to pack their own lunch boxes for school. In such situations, most children who feel loved, and trust their parents to be there for them when they are truly needed, will adjust.

TIME MANAGEMENT FOR WORKING MOMS

There is no general formula for time management because we all operate under diverse circumstances. However here are some basic tips that will be of mighty assistance to all mompreneurs

1. Review your activities. Take a good look at what you waste your time doing really. We spend at least an hour a day on activities that, if there was not enough time, could possibly be delayed or even entirely cancelled.

2. Set priorities. Most of us find it difficult to decide what is really important and what can just as easily wait. It is better as a working mother to spend five minutes at the end of a working day setting priorities for the next day than running around in a mess the next day and ultimately not really doing what needed to be done.

Try dividing up your tasks:

Things that have to be done immediately (or first thing the next morning after making coffee)

Tasks that can be done at any time during the week (but they have to be off the table at the end of the week!)

Things that have to be done again and again because they belong to long-term projects or are simply regular tasks

If that helps you, you can write the things on different colored cards.

3. Plan better ahead and set tighter schedules. The idea behind it: It has been found that people always need exactly the amount of time they have available for a task. So think about where you can save steps in the task to be done that are not so essential, but that cost unnecessary time. And prepare as many things as possible for the next morning in the evening.

4. Be Organized. Bundle important things in one place, e.g. in a filing cabinet or a kitchen shelf. The best thing is to have a folder for each child (each in a different color for the sake of clarity), in which everything really goes: from school stuff to medical reports. Then one for you,(private) and one for your partner. For things that affect all family members, we have an IMPORTANT folder, for example. Of course, you need folders for your business, even if you work from home and don't forget to put it in a particular place.

When it comes to phone numbers and class lists, the best practice is to copy them and have one copy at home and one in the office. You should of course store them digitally in an accessible place.

5. Simplify your plans for your meals:

    Menu preparing, food shopping, and then cooking meals are tough when kids are around and everything fails if you start a week without a schedule.

    Instead to make the weekdays smoother, have a calendar with a specified menu. Enable 30 minutes to allow you enough time to pick meals as well as prepare your shopping list.

6. Multitasking. Sometimes it makes sense to combine tasks. Why not help the child with homework while you sit around for hours in a waiting room? The others can learn something too ;-) And a headset for the phone can be helpful if you have to make a lot of calls. You can, for example, clean or cook. Just make sure that these are activities thatcan easily be combined together.

7. Asking for help. It doesn't hurt at all when you get help. You don't have superhero powers that you have to do everything by yourself. When things get tight again and you're about to go nuts, another mother might ask if she can run a few errands for you, and you will take care of her children for two hours on another day.

8. Involve the whole family. Sorting laundry, picking up things from the floor, setting the table - even the youngest ones will find chores to do. And even if it takes longer at the beginning than if you were to do it yourself: at some point it pays off. You don't have to start practicing when time is particularly tight.

9. Write it all down: there are a number of family calendars out there even if you have very big families. Hang it up in a good location. Ensure that you input both daily and unscheduled appointments. Keeping a Google Calendar for the entire family is a smart idea, too, but sometimes it's easier to have

a schedule you can touch physically especially for the little ones.

You should also hang a grocery list (with a pen!) on the fridge and a whiteboard (with markers that can be cleaned off) with lists of items you don't want to miss on the kitchen wall. If you like you can make it to be very wide. You can even hang a magnetic pin board where you put important notes.

10. Pack the emergency bag. And by that I don't mean the clinic suitcase. But a bag that is always ready at the front door and contains the most important things that you need on the go with your children: Depending on the age of the children, maybe wet wipes, diapers and coloring book (although wet wipes are actually used at any age can), but definitely have something to eat, mineral water and handkerchiefs. So: that you don't have to start hectically looking for everything when things have to be done quickly. Of course, you should exchange the snacks and eat them at home if you don't come outside so that the food doesn't go bad.

11. You are on the internet - use it too! Do online banking, pay your orders via PayPal or similar so that you don't have to laboriously transfer the bills. You can buy gifts directly online, and if you do have to go shopping in the store: research online beforehand to find out where you can get which parts at a lower price and whether they are in stock.

12. Keep order. "Everything in its place and a place for everything" still works .And everything goes faster with order.

13. Summarize things with the same "topic". For example, you can keep the whole family's rain gear in one place. Put new notebooks, plastic binders, erasers, etc. for the school children in a drawer. When you do this, you don't have to look for everything in the individual rooms.

14. Use baskets / boxes. It is a good practice to put a box in each room in which you can put toys, books, etc. Then it looks neat when things have to be done quickly. This of course contradicts the "Everything in its place" method a bit. But everyone can put them away properly when there is more time.

15. If you have space in the hallway, you can set up a box for each family member, put in the backpack kindergarten bag, scarves, hats, gloves

16. Cook larger quantities. If you're cooking anyway, why not double or triple the amount? You can freeze the other portions and serve if you need to go faster.

17. Set everyday targets that are attainable

    When it is too ambitious, your to-do list is pointless. What's the point of writing down anything if your activities will not be accomplished? We aren't and shouldn't pretend to be superheroes. Let your goals be realistic and achievable. Understand that once you have the opportunity and the space, you can still do more.

In summary, what you need to do is introduce your everyday routine with a few smart tips. And when you realize that you have generated some space for something different, make sure you do something wonderful and be kind to yourself. You need it.

OVERCOME PROCASTINATION

I f there is any group of individual that need to understand time management principles, it's the working mothers. Meanwhile in the art of managing time, everyone involve must understand what procrastination is and how it can be defeated. This is exactly what we will talk about in this chapter.

Procrastination refers to the act of failing to self-regulate, and still delaying what is planned to be done when the consequences can be expected to be harmful. Procrastination is a ubiquitous phenomenon. A survey shows that about 75% of college students think they are procrastinating sometimes, and 50% think they have been procrastinating. Procrastination will have serious negative impact on an individual's physical and mental health, where there is a strong emotional remorse, guilt, constant self-denial, belittle, accompanied by anxiety, depression and other illness, happen once state needs attention

FACTORS RESPONSIBLE FOR PROCRASTINATION

The specific cause of procrastination is unclear. One view holds that procrastination is caused by one or several relatively stable personality traits, and individuals may procrastinate in various environments and conditions; another holds that The delays are mostly caused by unstable factors determined by the environment.

1. Environmental factors

    The procrastination behavior of the procrastinator is related to the time pressure to complete the task and the temptation of entertainment from the outside. Procrastinators often have difficulty resisting the temptation of the outside world, especially the temptation of entertainment, which leads to procrastination.

2. Task characteristics

    a. **Task difficulty:** degree of difficulty of the task will affect individual procrastination occurs, the more complex the task, the more likely people procrastinate when an individual believes a task beyond their abilities, sense of control due to a lack of success, often use Delay the way to postpone or evade the task
    b. **The time limit incentive** rewards and punishments task time also affects the completion of the task. If the reward is timely, it will reduce the delay of the task completion time.
    c. **Boring tasks** for the potential boring, resulting in frustration and resentment of the task, it will first choose to avoid, if not avoided, will be postponed to face as much as possible.

3. Individual differences

    Irrational ideas: If an individual believe that motivation to avoid failure is higher than the motivation to succeed, the individual will tend to delay so as to evade possible failure.

Low self-esteem: When you are not confident of your capacity to work the tendency to procrastinate increases. People who have encountered major setbacks in their work and are not confident enough about themselves are prone to escape and continually postpone completing their tasks..

Anxiety: When the deadline is approaching, too much anxiety can cause capacity paralysis and induce procrastination.

Impulse: Impulsive people pay more attention to immediate work because of incentives and ignore long-term responsibilities; they are therefore more likely to procrastinate.

Perfectionism:. Perfectionism can be divided into positive perfectionism and negative perfectionism. Positive perfectionists will actively find ways to complete a task to achieve the desired results, while negative perfectionists will usually employ delay tactics to avoid failure.

THE WAY OUT

1. **Change your understanding**

   Procrastination is negatively related to some cognitive psychology, and these incorrect cognitions can be changed by some methods, such as using positive hints, increasing successful experience, and magnifying advantages to gain confidence; changing perfectionism to help procrastinators analyze and complete the task Benefits.

2. **Positive emotions and motivation**

   You can change your mood through proper rest, divert attention, relax and entertainment, etc., and obtains temporary positive emotions. You cannot escape from reality and ignore long-term interests and fundamental solutions to problems.

In terms of motivation, the task aversion in the nature of the task affects procrastination, so it is necessary to convert the aversion task into a favorite task or add some rewards.

3. **Enhance self-efficacy**

Enhancing self-efficacy can largely prevent delays. Encourage individuals to self-manage themselves during the task completion process, actively monitor their own behavior and assess their expectations.

4. **Play the role of the group**

Group atmosphere can provide members with a special situation, full of understanding, love, and trust. Changes in this environment will inevitably cause changes in individual behavior.

TEN THINGS TO KNOW ABOUT PROCRASTINATION

Procrastination is a stumbling block that hinders personal success, but it often appears around us. Here are some things we need to know about procrastination

1. Twenty percent of people think they are procrastinators. Procrastination is a way of life for them, although it is not suitable for it. This state is full of their lives. They can't pay their bills on time. They forgot to buy tickets for the concert. They wouldn't buy gifts until the day before Christmas...

2. Procrastination is not unimportant, although usually we do not treat it as a serious problem. It is actually an esoteric problem of self-regulation. Usually we all tolerate excuses for others to procrastinate, which is the root of the problem.

3. Procrastination is not solved through time management or planning. It can only be resolved through strong determination.

4. Procrastination is not innate. It was learned from the people around, but not directly. It may come from powerful tutors, procrastination may even be a form of resistance. In this family environment, the tolerance of the procrastinators from friends will encourage this habit.

5. Procrastinating drinkers will have higher alcohol demand. Procrastinators will drink more, which is a sign of problematic self-regulation.

6. Procrastinators lie to themselves. For example, "I would like to do this thing tomorrow", or "I can do it well when there is pressure", but in fact it is not the case. Another lie for procrastinators is that time pressure will make them more creative. In fact, this is just their feeling. They are spending time.

7. Procrastinators are constantly looking for pastimes, especially when they don't need to promise anything. Checking emails is a great goal, and such things become a way for them to adjust their emotions (such as fear of failure).

8. Dragging is not exactly the same. Three types of procrastinators have been identified

    a. **DELAYERS:** These individuals have a tough time getting started on any assignment. For all kinds of reasons, they put things off such as...

        • Busyness ('I don't have time right now to do that')
        • Self-indulgence ('I need to relax')
        • Misplaced self-regard ("I need to take time off !")

- Wrong frame of mind (now I don't feel like doing that; later I will feel more like it ')
- Late day blues (It's too late to start this today; when I'm fresh, I'll do it tomorrow)
- Tiredness ("I'm too tired")

b. **DISTRACTIBLES**: These are people who are easily distracted. They will easily opt for something that guarantee immediate gratification instead of facing their major assignment. They can be distracted by Food, Television, social media, movies, going to the mall, unnecessary phone call etc.

c. **PERFECTIONISTS:** Those that are getting bogged down by irrelevant details. These guys start a task, but they can't finish it because it's not flawless. It isn't considered ready to be seen or judged because... according to them

- People are going to assume it's incomplete.
- People are going to believe I'm inept.
- They're not going to trust me to do that again.
- With two more revisions, I can do a better job.

9. The losses caused by procrastination are huge. Health is one of them, and studies have shown that procrastinators are more likely to get sick. Procrastination also affects people's emotions and also destroys teamwork and interpersonal relationships.

10. Procrastination will change people's behavior, but it will not consume much mental power. This does not mean that an idea can be changed immediately. This problem can be solved by highly standardized cognitive behavioral therapy. Admonishing people who are procrastinating is as difficult as making people with depression happy. "Professor Ferrari believes that persuasion has little effect on patients with

procrastination. The key is to rely on your own determination to get rid of procrastination.

As a working mother if you want succeed at work and at home, procrastination is something that must not be mentioned around you any longer.

IMPROVE YOUR MARRIAGE

Marriage is not easy, especially for a mompreneur. So hard, occasionally, that we wake up and ask why we dare signed that damn sheet of paper. Working moms have a complex collection of obstacles to hurt a stable relationship. We have fewer leisure, more commitments, (usually) more stressors, more duties and, sadly, more distractions. Have you ever sat down and remembered that you just can't recall the last time you and your significant other went out on a real adult date? Or even— had satisfactory sex? Yeah, the challenge is not peculiar to you!

Sure, not all of the partners are a great fit. Some marriages are just not designed to bear the test of time, and that's OK. But if you're positive concerning your life mate and want to get the best out of your life together, here are some things every working mom should do to make her marriage stronger.

1. **Get your priorities right.**

   Business opportunities will come and go. I will excel at some and struggle with others. However my hubby is here for good, so he is my priority over all else. Any choice I make in business has to pass the "will-this-wound-my-marriage" test first. If a decision could damage my marriage, it's out of the table right away. It's not worth it.

What is the value of a woman having gained the entire universe, if she has no soul mate to share it with? Value your partner, please. Cherish him above all other assets, ambitions and accomplishments.

2. **When you are at work send flirty messages.**

   You're, yeah, working while you're at work. But during the day all of us can squeeze in a couple flirty messages and let your significant other realize that you are thinking of him. You can bring some spice to your work day with a quick text message.

3. **Watch Shows Together**

   Choose one TV show that you're just going to watch together no matter how long it takes you to complete the season.

   Many marital counselors and analysts believe that couples who watch Television together are happier and more dedicated. It doesn't matter the genre of TV show, but viewing series with solid love plots has an added benefit.

4. **Relax**

   Are you fortunate enough to stay in a place where it's legal to use marijuana? A host of research indicate that partners who together smoke, vape or otherwise eat cannabis are kinder and gentler to each other. They even have more fun, in my own opinion at least. What is better than giggling and cuddling together after the children are in bed? And if your encounter with college marijuana has made you paranoid, give it another try. You're an adult, smarter, more optimistic, worst-case situation, and you get to feel like kids again with your partner. Make home time home time.

5. **Be at home both mentally and physically**

Yeah I know that entrepreneurship is exciting and stressful, and it's difficult to turn off that part of your mind, but you have to. This is a daily challenge for me as my life revolves around the investment in child care that I own and the social real estate network that I support.

Your partner will know that you're not engaging in the conversation because your mind is somewhere else: thinking about the next big deal, the stupid customer, or the competitor who is gaining traction in your field.

Switch the mobile phone off.

Don't look your email inbox

Get a genuine chat at dinner that doesn't require a talk at jobs.

If your marriage is precious, grant it the time it needs, and your union will blossom.

6. **Involve your spouse.**

Finally, I think it's necessary to include my hubby as much as she chooses to be in my entrepreneurial ambitions. By accepting my husband's feedback, a variety of amazing tasks have been done.

Then he can see the inside of my life and come with me on a thrilling adventure of entrepreneurship. We will experience ups and downs together, reinforce our marriage and encourage us to hold on during tough times.

The presence of my hubby often helps me to outsource some things to him so that I can get more done. For instance, in our real estate investment sector, my hubby helps with the books and works with all of the contractors that operate on our rental properties. He also works with lawyers when we need to evict a resident, which can be an extremely difficult operation, but far simpler with his help.

Finally, if your partner has similar aptitude like mine, he will definitely have a completely different view of the problem you want to solve, and he may resolve any issue giving you headache without much hassle. I can't tell you how many times I worry about problems in my business, and only a few seconds later, my husband came up with a feasible solution.

7. **Have sex.**
   I'm sure we all have the tendency to complain when we are tired, but this is a point I need to emphasize. No matter how tired you are, don't run from regular sex, in as much you are not too tired to eat. I will talk about this subject later.

8. **Send a hot selfie to him**
   Text or send him a selfie in the midst of the day – pose for pictures, play with your hair, smile, something that's going to grab his eye. Whether it's sexy, he's not going to stop dreaming about it before he gets home.

9. **Leave encouraging notes.**
   Sometimes this technology made us forget the old school method of showing love and deep affection. Wouldn't it be very interesting for your hubby to find a little stick note on his laptop telling him how much you love him? That is exactly what Im talking about.

A surprise love note brings back all the emotions you had when you were dating for the first time! Here are a couple of short little Love Note ideas that will inspire anyone easily

You're helping my vision sparkle.
I love the way you kiss me.
You're such a great husband.
You're the greatest mate of mine.
Whenever I see you, my heart skips.
I'm so fortunate to have you.
I enjoy having more time with you.
I do enjoy our life together.

10. **If you are not fully happy sometimes, its not abnormal** The overwhelming majority of couples claimed that after seven years of marriage, they were not as happy with their marriage as they were when they first married. However, projecting an impression of complacency or perfection can create unreasonable expectations for those around you (including your children) and damage your marriage. It is easier for you to recognize that your marriage is not flawless, and it will have ample space for you and your wife to find a way out of trouble together. After all the first step to solve a dilemma is to let you have one, isn't it?

11. **Find new ways to surprise your partner.**
Other than conflict or financial problems, many experts agree that boredom is the main killer of modern marriages. It leads to restlessness, frustration, stealing and even arguments, maybe in the wrong attempt to inject something exciting into a rather predictable union. Instead, try small presents, spontaneous dinner dates after job hours, a relaxing weekend trip, or fresh bedroom accessories. Also, looking for new ways to impress your partner will make your partnership more fun for you as well. Give your spouse an unexpected treat.

12. **Avoid Mother In Law problems**

The easiest way to have marital challenge is the inability to avoid problems concerning your in-laws, especially your mother in law. Here are some tips that can help.

a. Slowly builds trust
    Rash, naive confidence can also backfire. Anyone who entrusts intimate details from their own life to their mother-in-law at an early age should be sure that the mother-in-law really deserves the trust placed in her.

b. Geographical distance is good
    Even if the relationship with the mother-in-law is good: once you move to her property,dont expect things to remain the same. Offence will be drastically reduced once you are geographically apart.

c. Draw boundaries
    Drawing a certain line of boundaries can also help in dealing successfully with the mother-in-law. Because in the end you will only marry their child. And that doesn't make her your mother too.

d. Activities together are better than gifts
    Certainly, gifts can be a step in the right direction, especially on the first visit. In the long term, however, joint activities should be in the foreground, because this is the only way to develop a trusting relationship.

e. Approach without prejudice
    Often the cliché of the evil mother-in-law, the monster-in-law, is omnipresent. However, one should approach the relationship without these prejudices. After all, you have a great mother yourself. Then why should the partner's mother of all people be fundamentally angry?

f.   Honest compliments help
Nobody wants slimy daughters-in-law or sons-in-law. However, honest compliments can break the ice. Most mothers-in-law, for example, cook remarkably well.

g.   Congratulations on important holidays
Never leave all congratulations to your partner. Then you will only ever appear as a marginal note in their thoughts, since your own child understandably comes first. However, if you write her birthday wishes yourself, the mother-in-law will quickly take you into her heart.

h.   Approach the matter with low expectations
Only those who approach their future relationship with their mother-in-law with high expectations can be disappointed. However, if you first limit expectations to the bare minimum, you will be pleasantly surprised faster.

i.   Avoid competition with your mother-in-law
Your partner's mother and you are not competitors. The love your partner feels for you couldn't be more different. So don't see your mother-in-law as a competitor, because there will always be room for both in your partner's heart.

13. **Dress up for your hubby**

As a wife and a mother, I think it's necessary to wear makeup and dress properly for your husband and family. You are both busy, and I get that. It's necessary, however for your marriage and your spouse.

Like most of us, our husbands operate in the world in the midst of dolled ladies, with their hair all fancied, nails colored and filed, wearing their mini-skirts or provocative dresses. It's a part of life. Even if they're not walking arm to arm alongside women like this, they're at least introduced to them on their trip by billboards, or simply women wandering about.

There's female appeal everywhere. And, sadly, for them most visual disturbances are aimed at men, being extremely visual beings.

Since we're wired differently, it may be challenging for a woman to understand. Why am I expected to go through the hassle of dressing up? My husband likes me regardless of who I am, doesn't he? He married me, after all.

That's true, ladies. However it's a smart thing to remind our husband that he's married. When you were dating, how did you introduce yourself to him? Have you been sporting sweatpants all the way with your hair drawn back, unlined, wearing flip-flops? Have you been dressing frumpy or attractive? How did you introduce yourself to him much of the time?

At least I realize that I've still got lipstick on and attempted to dress pretty attractively. I always liked this man, after all! He was quite a gentleman for me, he was a diligent worker, and he was very sincere (not to mention he was pretty good looking!). I needed him to do that because I wanted him to want me! I have been actively seeking to lure him.

Now, I don't think you're going to have to waste an hour every morning curling your hair, putting on your mascara, etc. However, I think y our husband just needs to see you looking good for him.

14. For each bad thing about your partner, find five good ones.

Write down a trait or action every time your spouse does something that irritates you . Then mention the five positive things for your partner on the other side of the page. They don't have to be associated to anything that is annoying. Instead of sending out an angry text in reaction to the dumb thing he just did, you'll notice that the anger is diminished by recording the good things, and before you know it you'll have a lengthy list of all the excuses why you married him

15. **Don't go to sleep without saying, "I love you."**

I'm not going to start telling you never to go to sleep upset with your spouse. That's unthinkable; it can hurt you medically and psychologically. No matter how angry you are, remind yourself before falling asleep to reassure your companion that you love him. p It's not always going to be straightforward, but both of you are going to sleep well, and more often than not, those three clear words are going to save the dispute from extending into the morning. Let this be part of your routine every night

16. **Communicate.**

You both are incredibly busy, so it may be a hassle to find time to chat, even if it's only about your snippy co-worker or an upcoming case. You ought to get your partner as an up-to-date sound board for the difficulties and tribulations of your life. And if the way to work is just 10 minutes in the morning, inform your partner as soon as you can about what's happening to you. The point is: as much as you can make sure you are communicating.

18. **Listen.**

    Whenever your companion is discussing his current business with you, listen. It's too tempting for working moms to let our thoughts wander to the next thing on our to-do list as our husband start a seemingly less important discussion They recognize when you're at faking it, even if you're totally there. Listening to others helps them feel respected and appreciated, and listening will make you a happy individual overall. The to-do list you are thinking about can still wait.

19. **Never stop trying**

    Marriage is not a math problem with a single, irrefutable solution. It's not also a poem that you can examine in three different manners to get three diverge interpretations. It's almost like an insane collage that you keep working on every year. The healthiest perspective is to recognize that your union will continue to be a work in progress. Besides who needs a perfect marriage? The adventure of life is all about falling down and rising up again, because every time we do it, we find ourselves tougher, smarter and stronger

YOU AND YOUR SELF ESTEEM

As a mompreneur there are many factors responsible for success and record-breaking achievement. Healthy self-esteem, your capacity to think well of your personal ability and worth is one of them. In this chapter let us look at the importance of healthy self-esteem and its relevance to a life well spent

As a working mother, who is expected to do well at work and perform adequately at home, we will all have to experience moments of adversity, which can become demotivating, however if our self- <u>love</u> is strong, we will be able to see beyond those situations and not be discouraged.

As a general rule, a process of change will always generate resistance. Nobody likes to make mistakes, or feel that things do not go according to expectations. However, high self-esteem is necessary to cope with disappointment and to adapt flexibly to any change, threat, or tragedy. This tool will help us to approach each crisis as an invaluable opportunity to learn, grow and transform ourselves; appreciating it as just a passing stage. We can react wisely and obtain better results, because instead of victimizing ourselves and thinking 'why me?', We will ask ourselves 'what can I learn from this?'

IT HELPS IN THE ACHIEVEMENT OF YOUR DREAMS

Having high self-esteem is important because it greatly influences the decisions we make. In other words, it has a motivational function that enables people to take care of themselves and explore their full potential to the uttermost. Those who have a strong self-esteem work persistently in the fulfilment of their personal goals and aspirations, while those who do not, tend to consider themselves as not worthy of happy results, or incapable of achieving them. They may still have ambitious goals, but they often lack the determination to make things happen.

An individual with high self-worth also has a high level of self-knowledge, that is, he is aware of his greatest strengths and abilities, as well as his limitations and weaknesses.

And with his shortcomings, he embraces himself as he is and understands that the most crucial thing is to associate with those that have such qualities that he lacks. He understands that operating with a team make one more successful and therefore continues to ask for support when needed.

HEALTHY SELF-ESTEEM STABILISES EMOTIONS

Just as there are different theories and studies on emotions, there are also on the types of emotions and the way of classifying them, being some more complex than others and none completely definitive.

However, we want to present a useful classification for you to learn to better identify the types of emotions we experience.

1. **Primary, basic or innate emotions**

These are the types of basic or innate emotions that we have in response to a stimulus, they are common in all human beings and all of them constitute processes of adaptation. These types of emotions are 6: sadness, happiness, fear, surprise, disgust and anger, although recently there is a study that says there are only 4 primary emotions.

1. Sadness

    Sadness is a type of negative emotion in which we make an assessment process about something that has happened; That something is the loss or failure of something that is important to us. This loss or failure may be real or probable and permanent or temporary.

    Something very interesting about sadness as an emotion is that we can experience it also if it is someone important to us who is going through that loss or failure. In addition, sadness may be in our present as a reflection of memories of the past or anticipation of what we believe will be the future.

2. Happiness or joy

    Happiness or joy is a positive innate emotion that we experience since we were born and that as we grow becomes a great source of motivation. This emotion is very useful in the first years to strengthen the bond between the parents and the child, a fundamental basis for our survival.

3. Fear

    Fear is one of the emotions that has aroused most interest in research on human emotions. This is the emotion we experience when we face what we consider a real danger and our physical or mental well-being is threatened, so our body reacts and prepares us to face or flee from that danger.

You should know that not all people live fear in the same way and it depends on each one what we consider danger or threat to us.

4.   Surprise

Surprise is a kind of neutral emotion, because it does not have a positive or negative connotation in itself. It is what we experience when something happens completely unexpectedly, that is, when an unforeseen stimulus appears.

Being an unforeseen, our body feels that it has failed in its attempt to predict the outside world, so it tries to explain to itself that unexpected stimulus to determine if it is an opportunity or if that event is a threat.

5.   Disgust

This is the emotion we experience when something generates disgust, so a tension arises that seeks to avoid or reject that stimulus. It is a defence mechanism that we have to protect our body, which is why nausea is often one of the answers.

6.   Anger

The last of the basic types of emotions is anger and it arises as a mechanism of self-protection when we are offended by other people, abused or when we see that an important person for us is the one, they offend.

2. **Secondary emotions**

   The types of secondary emotions are the group of emotions that happen or originate after the basic ones and are generated by social and moral norms learned. For example, when we experience innate emotion in the face of some stimulus, such as fear, and immediately afterwards we experience secondary emotions such as anger or threat.

3. **Positive emotions**

   Here we include those emotions that when we experience them positively influence our behaviour and well-being, which is why they are also known as healthy emotions. Our way of thinking and acting improves when we experience joy as emotion, for example.

4. **Negative emotions**

   Contrary to the type of positive emotions, when we experience negative emotions, they negatively affect our well-being and behaviour. They are also called toxic emotions and usually when we experience them, they cause us to avoid or avoid them. Fear and sadness are negative emotions; however, they are necessary for our learning and growth process because they teach us about the consequences.

5. Ambiguous emotions

   Surprise is an ambiguous emotion because it is totally neutral in itself and does not make us feel good or bad, so it is called ambiguous emotions.

6. Social emotions

   Are those types of emotions that we experience by the presence of another person necessarily, otherwise they do not arise, so we are not talking about learned cultural emotions. For example, gratitude, admiration or revenge are emotions that arise with respect to someone else.

With healthy self-esteem, the positive emotions like joy are established while negative emotions like fear, disgust, sadness and anger are suppressed!

SELF ESTEEM AFFECTS RELATIONSHIPS' SUCCESS

Researchers have identified the connection between high self-esteem and satisfaction with relationships. Self-esteem influences not just how we think of ourselves, but also how much affection we will get, and how we accept others, especially in interpersonal relationships.

The initial degree of self-esteem of an individual prior to a relationship predicts its happiness and satisfaction. More precisely, while happiness usually decreases marginally with time, this is not true for individuals who move into the relationship with higher self-esteem levels.

The steepest drop in the level of happiness is among people with a poorer self-esteem to begin with. These relationships just don't last. Although communication abilities, emotionality and tension are solid factors that affect relationship success, previous knowledge and personality characteristics of an individual affect how these issues are treated and therefore have the greatest effect on their outcome.

SELF ESTEEM AFFECTS MENTAL HEALTH

Mental health can be defined as the degree of psychological wellness or an absence of psychological disorder. It is the state of an individual who is performing at a normal level of emotional and psychological adjustment".

From the viewpoint of positive psychology, mental health can encompass a person's capability to be happy with life and to fathom an equilibrium between normal living routine and efforts to remain psychological resilient.

As stated by WHO, mental health combines Subjective well-being, presumed self-efficacy, sovereignty, independence, intergenerational dependency, intellectual and emotional self-actualization, among others". The World Health Organization further states that an individual's well-being requires understanding his or her ability, dealing with normal pressures on life, meaningful work and contribution to his or her society.

Study has shown that medically evaluated young adults with high self-esteem report lower levels of anxiety / depression and attention problems, indicating that self-esteem serves as a measure of resistance against such symptoms.

SELF ESTEEM GIVES A SENSE OF PURPOSE

It is relatively easy to be able to define your passion and intent, as you recognize and believe in yourself. This will not only give you happiness in the present, it will also enable you to prepare for the future.

Understanding and trusting in your talents, which is what healthy self-esteem is about, ensures that you are motivated regularly to go ahead in the pursuit of your professional and personal targets

SELF-ESTEEM AND RESILIENCE

Resilience is the psychological attribute that allows some individuals to be pulled down by life's adversities and to bounce back at least as powerfully as before. Rather than enabling challenges, stressful incidents, or loss to conquer them and sap their determination, extremely resilient individuals find a way to switch direction, recover mentally, and strive to progress towards their objectives.

People with high self-esteem are very resilient and won't allow themselves to wallow if things don't work out as scheduled. For who they are, they recognize that failure is part and parcel of the journey of life. As such when they fail, they easily pick themselves up, forget the past and try again and again. They have the faith to assume that eventually all will be well.

SELF ESTEEM WILL DETERMINE YOUR SUCCESS AT WORK!

You are certainly spending much time in your professional life, though you are trying to cope at home too. You're getting ready for work, commuting to work, doing your job all day long, having lunch with colleagues, coming home from work, changing from business wear to more comfortable attire, and attending to kids and hubby and getting ready for the next day. Having a good sense of self-esteem at work is often essential to a stable and rewarding career.

Your relationships with the leaders and your co-workers in your workplace can make or break your work experience, particularly when it is difficult. By thoroughly knowing others' core interests, you can figure out what they want, and how they will respond. And all this will only happen if you have a positive self-esteem.

OVERCOME YOUR GREATEST ENEMY!

As a working mother, the greatest enemy of your self-esteem is what I call the inner critic! If you want to be successful in your roles at home and at work there are some things you need to know about this INNER CRITIC—the voice of your mind that keep analysing your faults and shortcomings.

1. It's not on your side

    Your inner critic generally keeps a magnifying glass on the smallest mistake, flaw or element of self-doubt. If he discovers one, he uses the flaw as an excuse to dismiss you as a whole person, to write you off as a pitiful loser. Are you going to accept this from a friend? Would you like to share time around someone that tells you that the reason you thought today was a 'no-uniform day' at your children's school is that you're a stupid bimbo that can't get it right?

    Your inner enemy would never use the magnifying glass to show what you have achieved right, or your talents and abilities. Like any single human on this world, you are a blend of good and evil, abilities and disadvantages, skills and shortcomings. Yet the inner enemy is reviewing the negative points and is poised to judge you on the grounds of the slightest error or slip-up. Imagine working for a supervisor like this one! How long will you stay until you quit, or at least start searching for another job? A week, huh? A month, huh? Six months, huh? And all of us have been up against a furious inner critic for ages.

2. It holds you back

    Imagine you have a seven-year-old son and he decides he wants to learn to play cricket. You have a choice of two local clubs to send him to – one that's run by Jeff, and one that's run by Neil. Jeff never lets up on any boy – he's always on their case, telling them what went wrong, picking out every tiny mistake. He's a stickler for detail. He regularly gives the team a dressing down for general behaviour, for being lazy and unfocused. He believes that if he lets go of his tight rein even for a second, the boys will start to slack off. Neil, on the other hand, believes in positive encouragement. He points out what went well before he talks about where there's room for improvement. He has a knack of noticing a particular talent in every boy, and helping them make the most of it. He believes in regular pep talks and thinks boosting the boys' confidence is the key to keeping them motivated. Now, which of the teams would you send your seven-year-old to? Which approach would you imagine would bring out the best in him, and nurture his enthusiasm?

Many individuals develop faster and learn more when compensated, congratulated and supported for their achievements than when blamed and disciplined for their mistakes.

3.   It blocks learning

Far from helping you to overcome problems, your inner critic prevents you from thinking clearly about yourself and your life. As well as zapping your motivation and making you feel discouraged, it prevents you from taking the 'objective' view you need to learn from your mistakes. By discounting your successes, and magnifying every mistake or problem, you lose the opportunity to learn from what went right, and get a clear and constructive view of what you genuinely need to change.

4.   It ridicules you when you're low

Not only does your internal critic weaken your morale and render you more vulnerable to depression, anxiety, or fear, it continues by blaming you for feeling this way, convincing you that you are worthless for feeling terrified, helpless, or sorry.

It makes you feel ashamed for feeling these things, or feel that there's something wrong with you.

There is still a lot of shame connected to anxiety and depression but the fact is they are somewhat normal disorders that should be viewed as a rather natural response to such life experiences.

Shameful feelings can easily be caused by stressful events, relationship problems or childhood issues. You're certainly not the first person to feel this way and you won't be the last. As such when next the inner critic attempts to knock you out of the ring of life through terrible accusations, don't agree with him and never fall into the trap of criticizing yourself.

5. It lies to you

    When things go wrong, in addition to criticising yourself for what you did, you probably tell yourself you should have acted differently. Perhaps you're right in thinking that acting differently would have been in your best interests. But in reality, chances are you had good reasons for acting as you did, even if in the end your course of action turned out to be misguided. (Maybe you were feeling stressed or tired or had too much on your mind, maybe you didn't have the help you needed, or were misinformed about a situation.) Your critical inner voice lies to you and tells you that it was obvious what you should have done, and the only reason you couldn't see that was because you're just so stupid. By blocking your ability to see a situation objectively, and using any setback as a stick to beat you with, your inner critic is stopping you learning from the situation and moving on.

    What should you do about your inner critic? Shout him down. Write down things you are doing right and read it loud. Don't let any inner enemy of progress reduce your self-esteem, hinder your progress and steal your joy!

SELF ESTEEM IN THE MODERN WORKPLACE

Research shows that the more roles people play, the more self-esteem they have. For a long time, meaningful work has been one of the important ways to make yourself feel good.

But where work is traditionally a source of self-esteem, this connection is now threatened. The one thing most likely to suffer damage in today's workplace is exactly what most of us want to get there-self-esteem. There are some huge psychological hazards in the modern workplace.

There are many ways in which self-esteem can be frustrated at work. The pace of work is so fast that no one stops to commend even outstanding performance. The demand for productivity is growing so fast that no one feels that they are doing enough. Everyone is looking at the unfinished workload and feels insufficient. We have unprecedented working hours. No one can keep in touch with friends and family again.

The resulting pressure will lead to a real increase in aggression and rude behaviour in the workplace. Rudeness anywhere makes people feel devalued! As a result, the workplace is no longer a place where people can have their self-awareness enhanced. Instead, it has become a major source of stress and frustration.

Maintaining self-esteem is a neurological mechanism that continues throughout life. Think of self-esteem as a muscle of the mind that needs to be built and sustained by daily mental activity, otherwise you would be vulnerable to depression and anxiety. At every point of life and every area of knowledge it has to be renegotiated. When we develop in-depth self-esteem within ourselves, whatever happens around us, we will learn to like and appreciate ourselves.

In a constantly changing world, the modern workplace is seen as containing some psychological stress. Whether it is a demanding work rhythm, lack of recognition of hard work, endless working hours, or competition for productivity, high pressure at work consumes one of leisure and family time, which is the therapeutic area of life.

We know that competence is essential to success in the workplace, professional achievement and personal satisfaction. But without confidence, skills can only take us so far. We are the harshest critics, and no one works as hard as us. People with low self-esteem will be presupposed by these critical voices in our heads, which will make him/her feel not good enough, hesitate, dislike, unworthy or even hopeless.

As people, no matter how broad these constraints can be, we generally do not go outside our own views. When we carry out day-to-day activities at work, there is a stronger unseen force behind our actions. People with low self-confidence typically do not embrace obstacles outside their comfort zone, and people with high self-confidence do not have the need to live in their comfort zone. In order to progress in your profession, you typically need to get out of your comfort zone and expand your boundaries to a new level of career.

Doubt about your own abilities, believing that others are better than you, or thinking that you are not doing well are common examples of low self-esteem at work.

How you feel about yourself directly affects your productivity and job performance, which in turn affects your career success. why is it like this? As you grow, you begin to experience and understand the world around you. You are deeply influenced by your parents, friends, surroundings and experiences. Over the years, most of their beliefs in the world have become their own beliefs.

These beliefs affect your thinking, how you think and think about things, and how you feel about things. The actions you take in life are governed by these feelings and emotions, so your actions will cause you to develop habits and life results. If you lack confidence in a certain area, there will almost always be a certain limiting belief, which is hidden somewhere and makes you unable to extricate yourself.

HOW STRESS AFFECTS WORKPLACE SELF-ESTEEM

Stress can be the consequence of workplace dynamics. It manifests in the form of changes in attitudes towards work or colleagues, decreased job satisfaction, tiredness, rude or aggressive attitudes, challenges to authority and other forms. Poor self-esteem often leads to fear of new and unfamiliar things, and can lead to unproductive work behaviours such as defensiveness, excessive obedience or rebellion.

There are different types of workplace stress:

1. Burnout

    You know that you feel exhausted at work and physically and mentally, and you continue to feel that your performance is not satisfactory. One reason for exhaustion is that regardless of your performance or effort, your boss will make you push you harder and criticise you

2. Acute stress

    Many workers experience intense pressure from time to time. This is a short-term stress caused by an uneasy situation. Once the particular situation is dealt with the usually accompanying pressure will disappear. For example, in the days or hours before the deadline is tight, you may feel a lot of pressure, but once the task is completed, you will feel relaxed.

3. Stress based on fear

   Due to the toxicity of your boss, or even fear of losing your job, you may also experience stress at work. When the boss does not like you, work may become very unpleasant. Some symptoms of fear-related stress include anxiety or restlessness. Yes.

4. Overwork Stress

   Due to the tendency to be a workaholic, overwork may be spontaneous, or it may be that employers continue to pile up work tasks with unrealistic expectations and/or deadlines.

5. New work pressure

   As a novice in the office, almost everyone feels uneasy. You must pay attention to what you say, what you do, and even how to dress.

6. Workplace conflict pressure

   Some of the workplace conflicts you will encounter are gossip and bullying. It is not abnormal in any organization.

7. Time pressure

   When it seems that time is not by your side, you usually face time pressure. If your work environment does not seem to have enough time to complete the tasks that need to be completed, and you are worried that you will not be able to meet expectations, then you will feel very stressed.

8. Anticipated pressure

   This stress is concerned with getting worried about the future. This may be precipitated by certain events, such as performance reviews or company introductions.

9. Encounter stress

    When you are eager to interact with someone or a group of people, you experience stress. For example, you may want to meet with the CEO of your company because you want to impress people. Otherwise, you may feel pressured by meeting a colleague, who is often mean.

HOW IMPORTANT IS SELF-ESTEEM IN THE WORKPLACE?

The actions of individual employees can create or destroy office space. Employees with low levels of engagement will reduce work efficiency, while caring and empathetic team members can help their colleagues through difficulties. Although many leaders want to view their organizations as well-functioning machines and objective workers, in reality, they rely on the emotional and mental state of their employees.

One of the factors that can determine the success of a team or organization is employee self-esteem. Without it, team members can't even complete basic tasks, and colleagues lash out at each other in fear.

Low self-esteem not only makes individual employees shrink. It has the power to spread negative emotions to colleagues, leaders, and subordinates until everyone in the organization is immersed in harmful thoughts.

"Low confidence makes us doubt our ability and judgment, and prevents us from taking planned risks, setting ambitious goals and acting on them,"

"At work, people with this problem often engage in subconscious behaviours that can undermine their success and make them less likely to request or get a promotion, raise or even work."

Employees who lack self-esteem often create a hostile work environment to compensate them. They list some common behaviours of employees with low levels of inferiority that you might recognize among employees.

Withholding: Failure to provide information, compliments or feedback to others to maintain an advantage.

Teasing and sarcasm: Comments may make team members laugh, but may actually stab the people they follow.

Breaking boundaries: Due to low self-esteem, eavesdropping, attention and asking too personal questions may be related to hostile expressions.

Negative self-talk: When your self-esteem is low, no matter what you achieve or how people think you are doing, tell yourself that it is not good enough. When you keep letting go of your footsteps, you will believe it and begin to appear less confident.

Hiding under the radar: When your self-esteem is low, you don't want to attract your attention and tend to hide under the radar. However, not being seen at work will keep you hidden, especially when you need a promotion and a raise.

Afraid of taking risks: Companies and companies want people who are independent, willing to take risks, and daring to innovate. When you feel inferior, these are the things you don't want to do. You are less confident and unlikely to take risks. You don't want to try new things, so as not to mess up the appearance. Without risk, there is no gain.

Workaholic: Sometimes, low self-esteem at work can turn people into workaholics. They never think that what they are doing is good enough, and they will continue to pursue better. They go to work early. They stay up all night. They overexplain themselves and devalue their work in front of others.

Pessimism: People with low self-esteem often feel pessimistic. They always look at the dark side of things and emphasize mistakes rather than accomplishments. When meeting with supervisors and colleagues, people with low self-esteem will point out their mistakes rather than accomplishments.

What Mompreneurs Can Do to Promote Positive Self-Esteem in The Workplace?

As a mompreneur, it is not only necessary to have a high self-esteem in your team, but your own self-esteem must also be very high. As an entrepreneur, you must encourage thoughtful thinking. Make sure you interact with the entire team. Some people will naturally make their own contributions, while others will sit there quietly and continue learning. This does not mean that their workload is reduced or the quality is not as good, but quiet employees often miss compliments because they are not yelling. Take some time to thank each member of the team, and give praise when appropriate.

THE FIVE FACTORS THAT MATTER

Here are the five factors that matter when it comes to making employees love and willing to stay productively in a typical workplace without losing self-esteem and relevance.

People

Employees respect cooperation and communication and expect to work in a environment that encourages collective communication. Employees said that as problems emerge, they want colleagues to support each other and to solve problems together. Communication with organization personnel is another significant factor. Employees want open communication networks in which they can easily exchange knowledge, learn from each other and get feedback in a constructive and positive manner.

Ethics

Employees are interested in working in a place that values fairness, dignity and ethics. Employees continue to work at an organization that retains its values. Honesty is a very critical quality that workers respect. It is also not enough for one organization to claim that ethical behaviour is respected. In its day-to-day corporate operations, the corporation must illustrate that its relations with all customers can conform with ethical principles and be accepted. Every worker should support each other's views. Diversity is to be respected. Employees will tend to collaborate with friends and managers who are trustworthy and accountable for their acts.

Respect and Appreciation

Employees want to be appreciated and recognized for their achievements in the workplace. They want to work in an environment where they are respected, trusted and listened to. Different opinions should be respected, and contributions to team projects should be valued. The company should not damage each other's credit. Instead, honour should be given to all team members. People generally expect that the workplace should be fair and supportive.

Positive Future

Employees want to work in a place where work and hard work are valued and processes are established. They can focus on customers and work towards a common goal. Employees hope their colleagues and bosses are willing to work for the common interests of customers and the company.

Achievement

Employees want to operate in an environment where commitment and diligent work are respected, systems are in order, and they can concentrate on the client and collaborate for common objectives.

Employees expect their co-workers and managers to be able to work tirelessly for their clients and the general welfare of the business.

SELF-CARE AND WORKPLACE SELF-ESTEEM

Caring for yourself (self-care) is the secret to good self-image. The more time you spend concentrating on your body and mind, the better you feel about yourself. And the resulting self-confidence will reflect in your behaviours. Regular reflection on factors that may affect your self-esteem in the workplace, and reviewing your strengths and assets may also be helpful. Welcome good deeds, but trying to please others may adversely affect your mental health. If saying "no" can help you maintain your emotional health, then it is not a bad thing. Setting healthy boundaries and disagreeing with things that don't fit your plan will only make you feel more "in control". Experts often suggest setting up some small tasks for self-challenge at work. It serves as a strengthening mechanism after receiving a small amount of rewards after completing each task. Find what you like to do, and then do more. Focus on "small victories"-don't pursue major achievements. Start celebrating achievements and also accept mistakes, receive praise, promote constructive ones and respectfully focus on shortcomings while ensuring a good work-life balance.

7

DON'T SABOTAGE YOURSELF

Juan is a mompreneur with two kids and a stay at home husband. The kids are growing the bills are expanding. She needed to take a better job. On the day of the interview she suddenly decided she is no longer going without any cogent reason!

María is a working mum, she started a new project that can mean a significant change and progress in her life and family, but she never has time to finish it.

On many occasions, working mothers are involved in this type of dynamics. In certain cases, the circumstances do not favor her however, in most cases, the main obstacle is the person herself, who **for the fear of the unknown falls prey to self-sabotage.** Let's see what this phenomenon consists of.

WHAT IS SELF-SABOTAGE?

Self-sabotage and all those behaviors that are related to it, are unconscious acts that appear at times that can be a great change in people's lives, whatever type. These behaviors **tend to hamper**

the achievement of goals or achievements through unconscious self-manipulations.

The goal of self-sabotage is to **keep the person in their comfort zone**, within which everything is easy or, at least, predictable. It is also a type of unconscious defense mechanism through which the person tries to avoid possible future suffering, stressful situations or unknown situations.

CAUSES OF SELF SABOTAGE

There are a lot of possible causes of self-sabotage. Taking these causes into account, it will be easier for everyone to avoid them and thus more easily achieve what is proposed. These causes can be:

Having **trouble prioritizing objectives**.
Lack of self-control.
Lack of motivation or high pressures during childhood.
Not really knowing what you want to achieve.
Low self - esteem.
Lack of self-confidence.
Limiting beliefs that the person does not deserve their own success.
Objectives imposed by third parties.
Fear of failure.
Fear of change and leave the comfort zone.
Internal conflicts.
Fear of not living up to the expectations of others.

All these signals, beliefs and traces that inhabit the person's mind appear unexpectedly, acquiring control over the person and their behaviors and **interfering with the projects and possibilities of evolution of the person**.

Self-sabotage is a manifestation of all those aspects that the person fails to accept from himself, all those beliefs based on fears and that, over time, by force of not being confronted, have gained weight and power within it.

Therefore, these obsessive thoughts and harmful behaviors are only **a symptom that there is something deep in the thought that must be examined**. Although in many occasions, delving into these thoughts is not pleasant, this evaluation of oneself can be an opportunity to move forward and to learn to face any future situation that may arise.

CHARACTERISTICS OF SELF-SABOTAGE

There are a series of defining characteristics of self-sabotage, which allow it to appear before certain situations but not before others. That is, a person who unconsciously self-sabotages when facing a certain aspect or circumstance of his life does not have to do so in everyone else.

These self-sabotaging behaviors **appear above all in situations that involve a great responsibility** or when the person must make an important decision which will imply some kind of change in their life.

Symptoms or manifestations experienced by a person who is prey to self-sabotage include:

Intense fear
Insecurity.
Feeling of lack of control.
Self-suspicion or **lack of self-confidence** .

However, it is perfectly normal for the person to perceive all these sensations when they are about to suffer some kind of change in their life, it is something that everyone experiences to a lesser or greater degree.

The main difference between people who self-sabotage and those who do not, is that those who do **get carried away by fear and their beliefs that they will not get it**, while others are able to leave behind these fears and of overcoming all the thoughts that generate insecurity.

The most important thing when dealing with any kind of eventuality or transformation is not to avoid or avoid this fear, but to **be aware of it and act in a consistent manner**, without letting it invade our mind.

When the person becomes aware of both their fears and their own beliefs, in many cases irrational, it is much easier to choose the right decisions and avoid sabotage actions that stop or obstruct their aspirations.

TYPES OF SELF-SABOTAGE

There are four kinds of self-sabotage, which **are classified according to the type of behavior that the person carries out** .

1. Non Finishers

    In these cases the person starts a large number of challenges or projects which he ends up leaving halfway or even abandoning. Usually, the person tends to devote numerous hours of work and effort, and then give up when he is about to get it.

    The explanation found for this phenomenon is that if the person does not finish this or any other project, **he will never have to face the possibility of failure** or not knowing how to live up to the subsequent demands that this success will bring.

    However, what really happens is that it will never be aware of its potential, and at the same time it will be perceived as a mediocre person without competences.

2. Procrastination

Procrastination is said to be the art of postponing things. **It consists of the habit of postponing** or delaying those activities that the person must necessarily attend, replacing them with less significant or more simple and attractive ones.

This habit is one of the most common within the population, and the reasons for carrying it out are the most varied. Some of these reasons may be that the person does not really like the task to be carried out or, and this is the most widespread reason within the scope of personal and professional projects, **that the person experiences a fear of the final result** .

In this way, if the person is postponing the completion of the task and does not invest all the necessary efforts and resources, he will have a justification if this is not as he expected. In other words, if the person devotes all his time and effort to achieve something and still does not achieve it, he will show his alleged incompetence, therefore if he does not try this it will serve as an excuse for failure.

3. Perfectionism

There are two possibilities within the excuse of perfectionism. Either the person thinks that since he cannot do something perfectly, he does not do it completely, or that through constant revisions and changes he avoids finishing the project.

4. Excuses

In addition to all of the above, the person may find a large number of excuses that justify **not facing any change or possible risk**. These excuses can be lack of time, financial resources, age, etc.

AVOIDING SELF SABOTAGE

We all have positive and negative experiences every time we have wanted to achieve something in our personal or professional life. On many occasions, we fail to reach our goals or objectives, with the bitter feeling of knowing that we are not fulfilling our purpose and of staying at the beginning of what could have been an exciting journey. Avoiding self-sabotage is not easy, but it is necessary if you want to be your best version ...

Self-sabotage is part of the human being as we know it. Somehow, growing implies change, and change implies discomfort, leaving the comfort zone. It is normal that we have a lot of resistance to that growth, and that is why we avoid ourselves to fulfill some of our desires.

When did you want to get something and you couldn't?

How many times have you had the sensation of putting on the zancadilla?

What do you think is preventing you from moving in the direction you want?

On almost every occasion when we are not achieving our goals, we could say that we are committing self-sabotage

Why does self-sabotage occur?

There are many reasons that make us not to realize ourselves, not to be able to become our best "self." The most powerful reasons for not reaching our goals have to do with our self-concept, with "who we think we are." Self-concept is formed throughout life, since we are born.

Our personality is mainly formed in childhood that is when almost all messages of capacity or disability, security or insecurity in oneself remain impregnated to us. From that early age, we tend to believe that we are in a certain way, and we are strengthening this concept throughout the years in adulthood.

In this way, it is common for a person with a great feeling of failure in his childhood, to create throughout his life that he is not very capable of achieving ambitious goals in life. Although it is also true, that the character can be changed and modified, and if one is aware of the limitations that are imposed, one can also stop self-limiting.

Our beliefs about ourselves determine our results.

The strongest beliefs are what we call "the script of life", that role that, without realizing it, you are playing since you were born. There are people who play a role of failure and prevent themselves from succeeding, others are invisible, others who are saviors, others declare themselves victims ... Each person assumes a role in their life from the moment they are conceived (the latest research shows that the feelings of the mother influence the personality of the fetus) and throughout his early years, and this role will be played by the person throughout his life ... unless he changes it when he reaches adulthood.

For this reason it is convenient, to avoid self-sabotage, to be aware of the beliefs about our identity that we can have, of the "I am" that we tell ourselves. On many occasions, when I listen to some people, I realize how many limiting beliefs exist in their mind, and consequently negative results in their lives.

Every time we say "I can't do it," "I never get what I set out to do," "I am introverted," "I am not a seller," ... we are somehow strengthening our identity with these kinds of limiting messages, and again entering a loop that will end up becoming a reality in our lives.

Henry Ford already said, "Whether you think you can do it or not, you are right."

We commit self-sabotage in multiple ways, there are many insignificant and significant acts we do every day to avoid getting really important:

> We avoid doing the important thing, putting ourselves first to do the least important.

> We look for the excuse of "I don't have time", every time we have to do something we would like.

> We turn off our anxiety by eating more than the bill or with some addiction instead of facing our own inner emptiness and overcoming it.

> We say "I will try" instead of "I will" ...

> ... And we fill our life with "should ...". By the way, all "would" and "should" are things we don't feel like doing.

How To Avoid Self-Sabotage?

Since the self-sabotage is part of us, the first thing to do is recognize it, admit the fact that you have thrown yourself thousands of times in your life. That you yourself are the most responsible for not having achieved the goals you set.

Once you decide to take the helm of your life, it seems that everything is more authentic, that a new world of possibilities opens up in front of you. In this world you are the main responsible, and you know that if you ropose, you will get it.

Once we have recognized our own self-sabotage, it is convenient to carry out healthy practices that prevent us from falling into the trap. I will show you some:

Energize yourself

On many occasions, the "I would like to" stay only in that because we have not been able to gather the energy needed to carry out our projects. In order for an intention like "I would like to lose weight" or "I would like to write a book" to become a reality, we have to start warming up.

When a soccer player goes out to the field, the first thing he does is warm up to go out on the pitch and do his best. This also happens to any of us, if we do not begin to energize ourselves, we will not be able to achieve what we set out to do.

To energize you have to:

Write about your goals and objectives. Use a newspaper and write down all your intentions, desires and dreams.

Tell others. One of the best ways to engage with ourselves is to tell what we propose to some people around us.

Make a small plan. To take away the fear caused by the unknown, the ideal is that we can outline what the plan would be, write it on paper and begin to gain the self-confidence necessary to begin the journey.

Start with a small step

Important goals are not achieved overnight. It is not a matter of a small action, but they are the result of many actions, efforts and attempts. For this reason, instead of setting ourselves directly with "the big goal," we could set small goals.

These small goals, have the objective of increasing our self-efficacy (how much we believe in ourselves) and therefore help us to change our beliefs or self-concept in order to align ourselves with our dreams and desires.

Thus:

> If we want to lose 10kg of weight, we can start by stopping sugar in coffee.

> If we want to write a book, we could start by writing an introduction.

> f we want to run a 15km race we could start by running 3km.

> If we want to increase our sales by 50% we could start with achieving two more orders today.

The Chinese aphorism already said "The longest path begins with a small step."

Start believing that it is possible

We have said previously that our beliefs condition our reality, therefore to change our reality we have to start changing our beliefs. Beliefs do not change overnight, they cannot be removed from the environment quickly. They are part of our personality, and anyone needs a place to hold on to face life, even if this place is their limiting beliefs.

Rather, what we need is to start questioning old beliefs and start replacing them with others that are somewhat more positive.

Any change we make in ourselves will provoke a response in our environment, for this reason if we change our beliefs a little, it will also change the response of our environment, and therefore we will begin to believe that a new reality is possible.

The person, who wants to achieve goals, has to watch their own thoughts to avoid self-sabotage.

The road will not be easy

No change was easy; every change implies some kind of discomfort. Changing means leaving our comfort zone and therefore finding ourselves in an unknown terrain where we feel insecure.

On many occasions we begin a path of improvement and we stay halfway. It is usual that we do not reach the goal because just after starting to walk towards our goals is when we experience more discomfort.

The most effective people in achieving their goals, are those who understand that the road will not be easy, and prepare mentally for it, so that when the difficulty comes they are prepared to face it.

Be aware of your tribe's influence

Your tribe is your environment, all the people and media that surround you. Our environment exerts a great influence on us, many people cannot change as they wish because they feel that their environment prevents it.

In a home full of unhealthy food it will be harder to change your eating pattern.

With a group of friends who love smoking, it will be harder to quit tobacco.

The others, our loved ones, have become accustomed to being in a certain way. So when we want to change, they will normally exert some resistance. The fact that you change forces them to change a little. Since in one system, if one of the parties changes, the other must also change to remain part of the system.

Although we cannot say that our environment is to blame for us not achieving our goals. Once we become aware of the influence of the tribe, we have to start operating differently to make our dreams come true.

So be prepared to hear saboteur messages from your tribe, from people who are used to being in a certain way. You will hear phrases like "don't change ...", "what are you going to do ...?" I liked you better before ... ". It is normal for the tribe to want you to be like before, that gave them a feeling of security and identity.

But don't be overwhelmed, people who really love you will never ask you not to change. They will invite you to fly, to grow and to make your dreams come true.

Look for balance

To achieve our goals and avoid self-sabotage, you have to feel well-being and peace with yourself. Well-being has to do with balance in the four planes or dimensions of being:

Mental Wellness: On the one hand you need your mind to have the maximum well-being, order and tranquility possible.

Physical well-being: A balanced diet, hydration and some exercise is essential. If you are not well, you cannot have the strength that is required to achieve goals.

Emotional well-being: A crucial point is emotional well-being. It is necessary that you get along with your feelings, that the affections and emotions do not overwhelm you. If you cannot feel good with those around you, you should make some adjustments in your relationship. In a toxic relationship people tend to self-sabotage more.

Spiritual well-being Regardless of whether you are a believer in any religion or not, spirituality tells us about the meaning of life, about the meaning of our surroundings. If we lose the meaning of life, we will surely sabotage ourselves when we achieve goals. Reconnect with yourself, with others, and with the unique feeling that keeps us all alive.

Avoiding self-sabotage is a journey towards yourself, a transformative journey, the only one journey that changes you forever.

THE TRAP OF STRESS

The responsibilities of a typical mompreneur are much. If she is not careful she may soon trapped by stress and become totally unproductive!

Stress is a social, behavioral or emotional expression in a medical or biological sense that causes body or mental tension. Stress may be external in nature (from the climate, psychological or social situations) or internal in nature (coming from illness, or from a medical procedure). Stress will cause the "fight or flight" reflex, a complex reaction of neurological and hormonal processes.

SOURCE OF STRESS

Generally speaking, the rapid development of the social economy has also created a sharp increase in stress. The sources of stress are also multi-faceted. There are three main reasons for stress: 1. work; 2. life; 3. personal personality.

1. **Working Factors That Cause Stress**

Dissatisfaction with work, heavy workload, and high job requirements are usually the main factors that cause work pressure. Especially when the remuneration received is not proportional to the individual's contribution, the individual is more likely to feel unfair and the pressure increases. Poor interpersonal relationship is another factor that causes work stress. Therefore, the first thing a professional needs to solve is to choose a job that interests her, such as opening a job to the market, serving as a professional broker, which is based on the talent's willingness to match the job.

2. **Life factors that cause stress**

There are occasional major accidents (changes) in the living environment, such as sick spouse, job change, new child, pregnancy, etc. that constitute stress.

3. **Personal character that causes stress**

The external environment and events do bring pressure to individuals, but the same events happen to different people, but they do not necessarily pose the same threat. Therefore, personal personality determines how individuals view stress events and how individuals cope with and regulate stress.

With respect to working mothers the major causes of stress are

a. Constant time pressure
b. Job demands
c. lack of recognition
d. Priority dilemma
e. Perfectionist mindset
f. Relationship difficulties with a colleague or a superior or spouse

SIGNS OF STRESS

The Harris Survey Center of the United States released information that 60% to 90% of human diseases are related to stress. Living under stress for a long time, your body will protest in different ways. In fact, there are several symptoms of physical discomfort caused by stress. In daily life, we can take measures to prevent and alleviate it ourselves.

Symptom 1: cold

If you feel exhausted and sore in the throat for several weeks, it is probably because the pressure weakens the immune system function, making the bacteria more easily invade the body and cause respiratory diseases.

Countermeasure: Pay attention to cold prevention measures, such as: drinking plenty of water, insist on washing your face and hands with cold water, and try not to let your hands touch your mouth, nose and eyes. Traditional Chinese medicines for preventing colds, such as garlic and Houttuynia cordata, can effectively protect against viruses in the early stages.

In addition, maintaining a happy mood is also crucial. For those who are prone to depression, walking outdoors often makes you feel better. It is better if you do more exercise.

Symptom 2: headache

Tension is the main source of migraine. Often, one in 10 women suffers from migraines of varying degrees, but only half of those with migraines will actively seek treatment. People have different opinions about the cause of migraine. Generally speaking, if you repeatedly feel pain and nausea around the eyes, it may be a precursor to migraine.

Countermeasures: First of all, you should not rely on analgesics, so as not to reduce the headache after medication. The correct approach is: take the medicine twice a week for a few months to form a regular, and then gradually reduce the number of medicines, such as once every 4 or 7 days; second, you can add some vitamin B2 to prevent; finally, pay attention to eat less Cheese, wine, nuts and meat food .

Of course, before this series of precautions are implemented, do n't forget to give yourself a long time sitting at the computer desk to have the opportunity to change the air and stretch your limbs, even for 5 minutes.

Symptom 3: Insomnia

Insomnia always worsens with increasing stress and burden. Other women are most likely to suffer from insomnia during their circadian cycle . The usual situation is: one to ovulation to lethargy, after ovulation, how could not sleep.

Countermeasure: Eat a small amount of turkey, cheese or tuna salad 1 hour before bedtime, drink a glass of milk, but do not eat sweets before bedtime.

If you still can't fall asleep, don't force yourself to do the game of counting sheep, it is better to get up and practice yoga. After experiencing the pain of insomnia all night, the remedy that can be done the next day is to find a way to take a nap at noon.

In addition, you can drink a cup of tea or coffee in the afternoon in order to keep up the spirit and continue to work.

Symptom four: herpes labialis

About 50 million people worldwide have herpes labialis. If you are in an overloaded state for a long time, the possibility of suffering from herpes on the lips will increase.

Countermeasures: When symptoms of blisters are found, first apply ice packs for 10 minutes, then take them away for 5 minutes, and repeat 2 times to suppress blisters swelling.

Symptom five: restlessness

Stress leads to lack of concentration and inefficiency in doing things. Forgetting to forget what you have just done, besides, it is easy to suddenly become sensitive to some ordinary things in your daily life, and render your negative emotions to those around you Over time, everyone will drift away from themselves, which will increase their interpersonal pressure.

Countermeasure: You can tell more about your stress to the people around you, or ask your friends for help. If you still feel the pressure, it is recommended to consult a psychologist.

HOW TO RELIEVE STRESS

Psychological pressure generally has three sources of pressure: society, life and competition. So, how should we adjust when we are under psychological pressure? Here are some methods for adjusting pressure (decompression).

1. **Exercises**

   Exercise can make the body produce the Philip peptide effect, which can delight the nerves. Peptide is a hormone in the body and is called the "happiness factor". The Peptide effect makes people feel happy and satisfied, and can even take away stress and unhappiness. Therefore, exercise is a good way to relieve stress and let people maintain a benign and peaceful attitude.

a. Learn how to exercise

To relieve stress through exercise, you can first participate in some moderate, small amount of exercise to calm your mood Then gradually transition to a large amount of exercise. This needs to be done step by step.

If the pressure comes from work and study, then you can participate in some group sports, such as basketball, volleyball, etc. In these sports, you can feel the pleasure of cooperation.

b. The choice of sports environment

The sports environment has a crucial impact on decompression. A good environment can make the effect more obvious.

For people who often exercise indoors, going outdoors to climb mountains and running in the woods will feel more relaxed and happy. In a quiet place, keep your eyes closed for a few minutes and take a few deep breaths to achieve the best relaxation and decompression effects.

2. **Meditation**

Through meditation, imagine your favorite places, such as the sea, mountains, etc., relax your brain; concentrate your thoughts on the "seeing, smelling, listening" of the imaginary things, and let yourself enter the imagination, just like your own In the middle, enjoying the spiritual relaxation.

3. **Dietary change**

Diet decompression is also a good choice. Many people will adjust through diet when psychological stress is high. If you are under great psychological stress, you may wish to eat the following foods:

1. Eat pineapple

    The pineapple is rich in vitamins b and c. They all have the effect of eliminating fatigue and releasing stress. In addition, the pineapple also contains enzymes, which can help the protein to be fully digested and broken down, thereby reducing gastrointestinal. burden.

2. Nibbling seeds

    Sunflower seeds also have a good effect of eliminating fatigue, because they are rich in nutrients such as unsaturated fatty acids and vitamins. Especially the zinc in it can also soothe emotions and eliminate fatigue. At the same time nibbling seeds can also relax your brain and get rid of bad emotional and psychological pressure.

3. Eat bananas

    There is a substance in bananas that can help the human brain produce serotonin, which can make people feel calm and happy, and they feel comfortable. The potassium rich in bananas can maintain the body's electrolyte balance and acid-base metabolism balance, maintain the normal state of neuromuscular excitability, coordinate myocardial contraction and relaxation functions, and maintain normal blood pressure. At the same time, bananas contain a large amount of magnesium to eliminate fatigue and relieve tension.

4. **Massage**

When your stress is too high, you can try a massage. We know that physical tension and depression can also lead to psychological tension and depression. When your body relaxes with a massage, your mental stress will also relax with it.

Apart from the universal solution to stress as emphasized above,a typical mompreneur can relieve stress by:

a. Intentionally taking time off all duties both at home and at work.
b. Accepting workplace praise and if possible demand for it.
c. Refuse to compare yourself with any other working mom.
d. Recognize personal limits and avoid perfectionism.
e. Visiting a psychologist or counselor.

IMPORTANCE OF ADEQUATE SLEEP

As a mompreneur there is always the tendency to evade sleep because of your workload. This is where you need to be extra careful so you don't end up hurting your business and career. In this chapter I will be talking about the relationship between adequate sleep and your productivity as a working mother

Friends and family are quick to encourage you to get a decent night's sleep," whether you have a major career presentation tomorrow or a marathon.

Sayings like this exist because, deep down, we all know how vital our sleep is to productivity. But for whatever reason, we still fail to figure out how to squeeze less sleep so that we can be more successful!

That's the other way around. You have to sleep well, not the other way around, to have more productivity. Keep reading to learn how bad sleep impacts your efficiency; while healthy sleep increases your productivity, and how you can guarantee that your sleep is efficient.

EFFECT OF SLEEP ON PRODUCTIVITY

Almost half of Americans complain that low-quality or poor sleep interferes with their everyday lives at least once a week.

Clearly, we are all conscious that insufficient sleep adversely effects our productivity. The more we operate, the more exhausted we become, and the more likely we are to making errors, to procrastination, or to the sluggishness that prevents our imagination.

Researchers noticed these results as late as the 19th century when they proposed reducing the working day from 9 to 8 hours, for a cumulative work week of about 40 hours. They could see that beyond that point, the quality of workers' production was severely diminished.

Many people work more than 40 hours, however, and even if you work a decent amount of time, the work cannot be efficient if you don't help it with a good sleep. According to the new efficiency and sleep study, "good sleep" relates to both the quantity and quality of the sleep.

PRODUCTIVITY KILLER #1: INSUFFICIENT SLEEP

Insufficient sleep is the first obstacle to productivity. Don't have enough sleep, and the productivity is going to struggle. You're going to have fewer resources and respond more slowly. You will become less imaginative and concentrated, and you will have trouble making choices and solving problems. These are the symptoms of sleep loss, and you will see that sleep-deprived people act out in the office.

In a broad 2010 survey, more than 4,000 employees were found in four major American companies. Unlike those who were classified as healthy sleepers, those with insomnia or poor sleep suffered the most serious efficiency deficits, investing about three times as much of their day on just time management.

Sleep deficiency devastates us both intellectually, physically and emotionally. When we don't have enough time, it's hard to concentrate through the day. We don't remember what we understand and take it. Our subconscious solidifies memories through REM sleep, but REM is focused in the later part of the night, because if we don't sleep sufficiently overall, we're losing more REM sleep than the lighter stages of sleep.

We often lose out on deeper sleep, the sleep stage essential for healing and rebuilding our muscles and body tissues. As a consequence, our bodies are more painful and we're quickly tired. In reality, one analysis of athletes showed that when you don't sleep well, you fatigue 11 percent faster than someone else. Long-term prolonged sleep loss is related to a number of severe health conditions, including obesity, type 2 diabetes and cardiovascular disease.

It's clear to see how the consequences of sleep loss adversely impact your success at learning, at work and in life. Being sleepless has the same impact as being high, and we all realize how unproductive we are when we are intoxicated.

Pull someone who was awake all night, and the reaction time is 50% slower than those with only 0.1 percent blood alcohol.

PRODUCTIVITY KILLER #2: INCONSISTENT SLEEP

Section two of the sleeping formula is regular healthy sleep. One research in 2017 tracked undergraduate interior design students wearing actigraphic wristbands, tracking their sleep patterns, and then offering them cognitive tests. The further erratic their sleep cycle, the worse their cognitive skills diminish throughout the week. These results have been verified by others, indicating that sleep regularity is almost as significant as the amount of sleep. A team of researchers have studied college students at Harvard for a month in 2017 and linked their sleep habits to their academic success. Both of the students in the sample received a comparable average amount of sleep, but those who observed a daily sleep routine fared far higher than those who did not. Those who got up and went to sleep at various hours had lower GPAs and delayed circadian rhythms. Their melatonin was emitted slower than the consistent sleepers, as though they had a jet lag, albeit without any flying.

This second research is at the core of why following a regular sleep pattern is so critical for productivity. Our sleeping period is determined by our circadian rhythms. Our circadian cycles adopt the day-night pattern ("-dian" is derived from "diem," the Latin word for day"). In line with that plan, our body produces melatonin in the evening, signalling to our brain that it's time to start sleeping. Our cortisol levels increase in the morning as melatonin decreases, waking the body and training it to face the day. If we don't adopt a normal sleep cycle, our development of melatonin is disrupted, because we don't fall asleep on time, and we feel the trickle-down impact that it has on the rest of our body operating.

Ignoring your own body clock has a significant impact on your efficiency. The prime example of this being night shift staff with reversed plans. Research on study reveals that certain people have performance problems ranging from reduced concentration and on-the-job mistakes that result in decreased efficiency to far more frightening effects such as drowsy driving incidents.

THE PRODUCTIVITY COST OF POOR SLEEP

These reductions in productivity are costing real money. In 2016, the RAND Company found that sleep loss costs the US economy $411 billion a year and more than 1 million missed working days.

People oversleep and wake up late, so they miss work entirely owing to sickness that they were more at risk of having when they were sleep-deprived. When they come to work, they're less concentrated and active when they're there.

That amounts to 11 lost days of production on an individual basis and $2,280 in lost wages per year.

Harvard researchers carried out several experiments focusing on sleep and job efficiency in the early 2000s. The more sleep-deprived subjects were around the board, and the longer they served with less sleep, the greater their chance of "fatigue-related errors," microsleep while driving, and injuries of drowsy driving.

Errors are bad no matter the profession, but in some fields, such as the medical sector, they are extremely serious for workers (one study found sleep-deprived surgeons are 20-30 percent more prone to error). Researchers claim that only by shortening job hours and enabling patients to get more sleep, medical mistakes may be decreased by about a third.

GET BETTER SLEEP AND INCREASE YOUR PRODUCTIVITY

The connection of sleep and productivity works both ways, thankfully. Much as bad sleep makes productivity worse, productivity improves with healthy sleep!

Get enough sleep, and you will reap the following advantages of productivity:

Speedier times of reaction
Better reasoning and skills in decision-making
Enhanced memory
Easier flow of imagination
Simplified problem-solving

Less mistakes and better precision
Decreased chance of burnout

You need to get good sleep, of course, to reap all these perks. And if you sleep sufficiently, if it's not profound, you won't enjoy the rewards. Individuals with allergic rhinitis, for example, have respiratory inflammation that impairs their capacity to breathe properly during night, so they suffer poorer sleep and diminished school or job efficiency.

Healthy sleep also encourages you to think straight. Many persons, like Einstein, Dali, and more recently, Larry Page from Google, claim that when they sleep, they had their best ideas. A good amount of REM dream sleep stimulates your imaginative mind, revealing whether you wake up from a dream-filled sleep with novel answers to difficult issues or with a brilliant new concept

HOW TO MAKE YOUR SLEEP MORE PRODUCTIVE

You ought to be sure that your sleep is healthy if you want to make your sleep more productive. Here are ten suggestions for becoming a good sleeper.

1. Find your best sleep schedule.

    What is the ideal sleep routine for productivity? bIt is determine by your nature and your chronotype. Aside from being a fancy term for if you're a night owl or an early bird, the chronotype determines your internal body clock, and whether you're more active in the morning or at night. Instead of attempting to push the chronotype to match social norms, lean on it and perform the best work at the best of times for you.

    Beyond the chronotype, you can still make sure that you get adequate sleep to stay rested. The typical optimal amount of sleep for adults is between 7 and 7.5 hours a night, although the optimal number for you might be beyond that range. When you wake up after 6 hours of sleep and feel fine, don't make yourself insane trying to push yourself to sleep for another hour. In the other hand, if you don't feel rested until you've had a complete 8 hours, acknowledge that and make room for 8 hours of sleep every night.

When you realize how much sleep you need, set a sleep schedule to allow that amount and observe it diligently. The more you prepare your body on a normal sleep cycle, the simpler it is to sleep and wake up. Meet this routine every day, including on weekends, to prevent any sleeping debts.

2. Induce sleep with a calming bedtime routine.

Any night, half an hour before bed, complete the same series of tasks in the same sequence. Typically we suggest up to 60 minutes, but because you have a packed day, we're going to limit that to 30 minutes.

The intention is to prepare your mind to equate this bedtime ritual with sleep planning, so as to strive for soporific behaviors if necessary. Take a warm soak, make a cup of bedtime tea, or write down your to-do list. Writing the duties down lets you clear them out of your head so that you can think about them tomorrow, instead of allowing them to occupy your mind when you ought to be sleeping.

3. Change your bedroom to a comfortable sleep environment.

Reserve your bed for sleep – no work, no hobbies, no binge-watching TV. You want your subconscious to equate your bed with rest and relaxation, not job stressors or entertaining TV shows.

Beyond activities, there's a lot you should do to keep your bedroom sleepy. Keep this calm and dark. Adjust the thermostat to a point in the center of 60 degrees Fahrenheit and use blackout curtains or an eye mask if appropriate. Top off the bed with a high-quality supportive mattress and luxurious bedding. Keep your bedroom tidy, avoid allergies and discomfort, and get rid of clumsiness, calm your mind.

4. Switch off your mobile

    Both devices mess with your sleep, so if you're like other people, your mobile would be your main sleep blocker. The issue with electronics and sleep is that both of these machines produce elevated amounts of solid, piercing blue wavelength – the wavelength of light that your brain perceives as being the highest and often synonymous with sunlight.

    The more your eyes drink in this sun, the more sure your brain becomes that it is daylight, and that you can be safe and awake. Plus, with smartphones, we prefer to keep them tight to our head, drowning our vision with blue light. In the meantime, we're always reading work emails or browsing Facebook, any of which may cause stressors on its own.

5. Level up your power naps.

    Everyone wants to get a rest at some stage. Why don't you invest that on a little sleep?

    By definition, a power nap is a quick 20 to 30 minute nap that is undertaken as a productivity boost. The brevity of the sleep is what makes it so soothing, so it's important to keep it brief. Much more than 30 minutes, and you risk falling into deep sleep, which makes it much more difficult to get up because you're going to feel more tired than ever.

It is also necessary to take the nap while you need it most, for example, during the efficiency dip about 2 or 3 in the afternoon. Schedule a rest, block the schedule, then go to find a comfortable spot to sleep in your workplace so you won't be judged. To take your nap to the next step, drink a cup of coffee just before of your sleep, then you'll wake up and feel extremely alert.

6. Get sufficient sunshine during the day.

    Sunshine wakes you up, but you could be wondering whether you might profit from more. The truth is that daylight helps to synchronize your circadian rhythms if you get a lot of natural sunlight during the day, particularly in the morning. During the day while the sun is out and sleeping at night when it's late, the brain is re-learning to be alive and alert.

    Pair early morning sunshine with a short walk or workout outside, use a light therapy box on your desk in the morning, or move your desk and chill outside the window and give yourself a special lift.

7. Regular Exercise

    This is another activity that also works to make your sleep easier, depending on what you do it. Speaking of exercise, don't function late at night because it activates the nervous system, making it impossible for you to relax. But exercise often and in the morning or in the early morning, and encourage the body to be psychologically tired out such that you almost fall in bed in the evening.

8. Watch what you eat and drink.

    A balanced diet provides for a healthy body to go along with it, and healthy sleep. Eat well during the day but be particularly mindful of what you eat in the afternoon. Limit the consumption of caffeine, nicotine, and medications. Watch out against for heavy dinners with unnecessarily fried foods, or sugar-filled late night snacks. They all screw with your nervous system and your mind to varying degrees, messing with your capacity to fall asleep and stay asleep. They can initially help you fall asleep, even with drowsy depressants such as alcohol, only to disturb your sleep cycle and wake you earlier than normal.

9. Wake up well, too.

    By ending productive sleep with productive waking, go for gold. Get out of bed and get moving on a morning routine that may include brushing your teeth, brewing a cup of coffee, or jumping jacks with some energy. Open the curtains to let the sun come in, or use an alarm clock for the dawn simulator.

    For at least a little bit, stop staring at your phone or texts, helping your body to react to the day a little before hitting it with tension.

10. Schedule tasks while you sleep.

    With all this spare time spent sleeping, if you're afraid you won't get anything done, brainstorm how you can plan those things to take place while you sleep.

    Using a slow cooker, cook dinner tomorrow. Schedule your red-eye work ride so that you can relax while you fly. Check the content before you sleep if you want to focus on solving a specific dilemma, or have a major test the next day so your subconscious can focus on it in your sleep.

Additional tips:

- Creating the ideal sleeping atmosphere, including illumination, colours, and smell.

- Their tendency to always overwork is a huge barrier to sleep and their success, considering what many workaholics say. Think regarding the particular challenges that impact workaholics and sleep.
- Losses of efficiency attributable to sleep are a real economic issue. Learn how badly sleep loss costs the world economy, and what certain firms are trying to solve it.
- Sleep, also the physical kind, impacts all efficiency. Athletes will hear about how improved sleep will boost their sporting success and render them an even greater opponent.
- Follow these ideas to boost your REM sleep and extend your aspirations to further innovative projects, whether you have a creative day job or just want to get more out of an imaginative hobby. Creativeness
- Identify your chronotype. Study the right hours to work and sleep for you, so you can change the rest of your life rather than disrupt it to facilitate your efficiency.
- In their paper, Sleep, Performance, and Public Safety, Harvard University discusses their studies on the correlation between sleep deficiency and injuries in the workplace or drowsy driving, as well as how lack of sleep impacts the capacity of the brain to operate properly, resulting in cognitive performance worsening.
- In a 2006 Harvard Business Review interview, Harvard professor and sleep scientist Dr. Charles A. Czeisler discusses the many aspects in which the ultimate performance killer" is inadequate sleep.

10

WORK-LIFE BALANCE

Women-owned companies in the U.S. alone have risen by 114 percent over the last 20 years. These trends reported in the 'Seventh Annual Study on the Position of Woman-Owned Companies in the United States,' can be seen as an indication that the field of entrepreneurship is finally accepting more women. Around the same moment, though these numbers might be more worrying for women themselves.

Many of these women experience obstacles when seeking to align their jobs with household duties at home. For all the debates on representation, women always perform much more jobs than men do at home. It places immense strain on female entrepreneurs and can have an effect on their success at the workplace. To correct these habits in every woman's life, they must fully restructure their everyday activities.

While the pursuit of work-life balance can often seem difficult, it can be done with the right mindset and versatility. To help you accomplish this we have mentioned ten tried-and-tested tips that will help any woman entrepreneur to create a healthy life.

#1. Have Realistic Expectations

It isn't always easy for a woman to develop a well-balanced life. There are times that her family needs care, and the business requires her to concentrate solely on certain tasks. This makes it difficult for her to prioritize the duties, especially if it is necessary for her advancement. Try to keep your standards adjustable if you ever find yourself in such a state. Avoid thinking that women must be able to attend to all things every time. This concept will take a great deal of tension off your neck and encourage you to find peace in your life.

#2. Follow Healthy Habits

Keeping your emotional, physical and financial health in a good condition is important. Your role as an entrepreneur will eventually get more stressful if you miss meals, feed at an inconvenient hour, or do not sleep enough because of the hectic work schedule. Entrepreneurs perform a lot of jobs most of the time and face endless losses. Since they can't speak to anyone about it, they fight quietly. I will therefore advise you to cultivate essential healthy habits so as to be able to discharge your duties very well.

#3. Set Boundaries

Many woman entrepreneurs feel that working around the clock can help them expand rapidly and help their organization. But it can actually lead to general fatigue and lack of sleep. So if you don't want to be frustrated by your daily activities, set limits on yourself. Be clear as to what you need to concentrate on, and do so without apologizing. When your goals are defined, you will focus exclusively on them without caring about the obligations of others.

#4. Give Time for Yourself

If you are unable to invest any "me" time, it impedes your creativity and therefore in the long run, hurts your business. Yes, even with this crazy life, remember to find some time for yourself. You can enjoy a day with your children at the spa, go for a dental checkup, or schedule an adventure. This unique period set aside for taking care of yourself would have a favorable influence on your lifestyle.

#5. Evaluate Your Schedule

To decide what's working and what's not always set some time to review your schedule. As life keeps continuously evolving, the tips implemented a year ago do not work today. So at least once in each year, you need to constantly assess your schedule. It lets you effortlessly maintain work-life harmony and therefore makes you incredibly profitable.

#6. Reduce Distractions

Staying away from those things that distract the job or decrease its efficiency is always a safe practice. Try to drive them away when you are at work, whether it's social media, or your phone calls. This strategy allows you to do your work in less time so that you can enjoy the majority of your hours with friends and family. Often, outside of those expected hours, don't work. Particularly, if you work at home, it's high time after working hours to change off your laptops.

In addition, you can choose as "un-bookable" at least one day a week where you don't engage in any interviews or take phone calls. This technique increases productivity and allows you the ability without any interruptions to complete important tasks.

#7. Ask For External Help

Often it's incredibly difficult for a mother to work full-time when they will still be needed care for their family and water their romantic alliance. This could include preparing children's meals, cleaning the home, teaching the kids, and going for compulsory family get together. In such circumstances whenever necessary, you should call for external assistance to help cover some of your tasks.

Don't be afraid to talk to a buddy or business associate for some support when operating your business. In your personal life, you should ask for guidance from your family when it's needed. Often it's impossible to do all by yourself, so dont be reluctant to request the assistance of your close ones

#8. Stop Unnecessary Comparison

Comparing yourself with anyone will always be counterproductive. You may find yourself matching your qualities, like strengths and limitations, with those of other woman entrepreneurs

If you do this often, ultimately your growth will be hindered. This emotional motivation is part of the fundamental urge to know oneself best in the universe, according to the principle of social contrast. But spending too much time doing it might hurt your self-confidence rather badly.Your duty therefore is to concentrate on your own objectives without unnecessary comparison. This will help you hit your targets and succeed.

#9. Learn to Say NO

Although it sounds frightening and wrong to say no to your supervisor or co-workers, it will really help demonstrate your dedication to the quality of your job. By saying no to certain things, and expressing that you do not want to lose consistency and optimum efficiency on your other tasks, you prove that you can keep your workload correct and that you are committed to delivering successful results.

If we cause ourselves to be stretched so thin, we're not good for anyone. We can't save ourselves, our loved ones, or do a decent job. It should be a high priority to respect our resources and time! We are not responsible for the responses of other people to us, and we are genuinely responsible for the satisfaction of just a few people.

#10. Technology Can Be A Real Advantage:

For woman entrepreneurs, technology makes life even simpler. The infrastructure is now in position to enable most entrepreneurs to work at least part of the time from home. Remote employment suggests that with their hours, business women can be versatile. When your child is sick or the babysitter is cancelled, you will find time to go to an appointment or stay home, without missing the opportunity to work. Of course, the flip side is that technology makes it all too easy for your home life to be disrupted by work. When you have one eye on your social media accounts, being constantly available will easily spiral into business calls at dinner, or not being completely involved with your children. For female entrepreneurs, technology is a blessing, so be careful to use it in a manner that helps the work-life balance instead of damaging it.

#11. Stick to Your Plan

You are more likely to be tempted to skip the guideline as a business owner or force yourself to work long for the annual targets to be accomplished. You must tell yourself to obey a rational timetable in those situations. After the end of the work schedule, you can unplug it and give yourself or your family more time. In addition, also consider sticking to the holiday timetable. With daily holidays, treat your entrepreneurial life as a 9-to-5 work. This technique will recharge your level of motivation and help you feel refreshed when you return to work. Overall, if you do not want to be overworked, be clear and set constraints in your professional life.

Make the most out of it!

It is never easy to take an entrepreneurial path. In specific, you can feel obligated, as a woman, to manage everything. But the fact is no one can do all of that alone. You have to learn to navigate your work and personal life carefully to lead a healthier life. So to build a working-life balance, avoid seeing it as your duty and follow the validated tips listed up here. It will give you, in exchange, a better and happier life.

WORKING WOMEN AND CLEAN HOMES

When you work full-time, attempting to keep your house clean will sound like breathlessly spinning on a never-ending hamster wheel of anger and dissatisfaction. But it doesn't need to be like that!

It's not always convenient to keep a tidy home while you work full-time. However there are a few things in common with career women who have a clean home. Here are 9 habits of clean-homed working people. When balancing a full-time job with your responsibilities as a mother these strong routines will help you keep your house tidy.

REMEMBER PRIORITIES AND HAVE REALISTIC EXPECTATIONS

Working mums don't get obsessed with how clean their home is, they are realistic and know the limit to how much can be done.

You should remind yourself periodically that you only have a little time to keep the house clean and set cleaning goals accordingly.

We clean the stuff that mean the most and are important to us and when we have any spare time and resources, we'll do the rest. According to what we are capable of, we run a household and don't care about what anyone else says.

Find and keep to a cleaning regimen that works

On every given day the last thing a busy, exhausted working woman wants is to try to determine what to clean. A basic calendar-based cleaning guide eases decision fatigue immediately, makes it easier to assign cleaning as appropriate to family members and helps you to establish a daily schedule. Using a cleaning schedule to build a regular cleaning habit, and the house can keep tidy even more quickly.

Clean and tidy up as you go

Savvy working mothers know that as they clean and tidy up all day long, they find life even simpler on their own.

.Don't misunderstand what I'm trying to pass across. I don't imply that all evening you must wear an apron and use all your spare time to clean and put away things! Below are few explanations of how cleaning can integrated into your daily activities:

Clean it up if you have a stain on the floor.

Note the dust next to you on the coffee table? Wipe it off with a dust cloth or a facial tissue

Every time you use the kitchen sink and counters, clean down

When you're passing by anything that has to be packed aside, dispose of it immediately.

We save ourselves lots of time cleaning down the path by spending a couple more seconds here and there to clean and put stuff away while we continue our normal activities at home.

Throw away whatever you are not using

It's crucial that you and your family remember to put stuff away once you're finished using them. For you to keep your house tidy, avoid leaving things you are not using again to gather dust, mess, and create further work for you. Get into the routine of throwing away dishes, toiletries, clothing, etc whenever you're finished with them and the home can remain cleaner and less cluttered.

Declutter regularly

You can also declutter on a regular basis, just like you can tidy and clean up as you go about your activities at home.

Let's assume you open your bathroom closet, for example, and see a ton of hair care items that you no longer need. What you should do immediately is to set aside few minutes and get them into the dust bin! Or if you see some old furniture that are no longer useful for anyone, don't waste any time, just pick them up and get them out of the house immediately

Keep an eye out for something you no longer want, use or enjoy when you walk through your house. You'll have less mess to contend with fewer things to vacuum up, and a happier, more comfortable feeling in your home by constantly arranging your possessions.

Keep those effective multitasking items ready for cleaning

Keeping your house clean is impossible if you don't have the cleaning supplies you like! A perfect way to derail your cleaning routine is to run out of product, but it's completely avoidable. In your house, you can always have a backup of each of your usual cleaning items on hand. Soon after you open the backup, a simple rule of thumb is to order or pick up a new bottle of the item

Always make cleaning an enjoyable event

Let's be real... few of us really like cleaning (yes, I'm one of the weirdoes who enjoys cleaning up). But do you know that washing doesn't appeal to me? And I make sure that I never JUST clean up.

I imagine you can think of at least 10 things you might rather do than clean your home. When you clean your home, why not do any of those things? Listen to music or a podcast, tote your tablet around and enjoy one of your favorite programs or movies, chat to a friend or family member on the web.

When you sweep, there are so many enjoyable activities you should do.

Secure the assistance of others in your household

Obviously you are not the only person living in that home that means you're not liable for all the mess in the house. Then why are you the only one who's struggling to keep things clean?

Most of the reasons that I don't forget to tidy up is because I've been doing this since I was 5 or 6. My mother served as a teacher all day and night, and also went back to school to earn a college degree while I was in junior high school. This means there is no way that she can be cleaning our house on her own! My parents therefore request me and my brothers to help with housework, tidy up the room, and take the lead in the laundry process.

You should assign cleaning duties to and family member – such as doing your own laundry, cleaning your own room/bathroom, unloading a dishwasher, etc. Once your spouse consistently helps in simple cleaning tasks, you would be able to concentrate on those tasks that make your home look pretty good. You're also going to be forced to breathe a bit!

Don't Allow Yourself to Be Overwhelmed

Often, everyone goes back to sweeping, or feels stressed, or has little energy. That stuff is natural. In order to control their response to such emotions and circumstances, career women who still have a clean home often participate in self-coaching.

Don't allow that inner critic to judge you. Keep yourself happy and motivated. Tell yourself that house cleaning is part of your struggle to keep everyone healthy.

In conclusion, it takes some effort to balance a clean house with a full-time career. However with the right routines and correct mindset you will make life better for yourself and keep your home tidy.

12

BE RESILIENT

To be a successful mompreneur, you cannot afford to be lilly livered. You need to be resilient. In this chapter I will be discussing all you need to know about resilience.

RESILIENCE DEFINED:

Resilience is the psychological attribute that makes it possible for certain individuals to rise again after they had been taken down by the adversities of life . Rather than letting challenges, stressful experiences, or loss overwhelm them and sap their determination, extremely resilient individuals find a way to change direction, mentally recover, and begin to push toward their goals. Resilience Mindset helps you to roll your punches and deal with what life throws at you. It's the capacity to adapt and come back when things don't go as expected. Resilience allow us to learn from errors and push on rather than wallow in the past or focus on the drawbacks. Being strong in some circumstances may also build up inner strength and raise trust in other aspects of life.

HOW TO DEVELOP RESILIENCE

It's not always straightforward for someone to get past pain and frustration without feeling downcast and defeated. Scholars have therefore gone ahead to investigate and ascertain what more resilient people do to move on physically and psychologically following the death of a loved one, loss of job, chronic or acute illness, or other common setback. The focus is to be able to encourage others to become more resilient themselves.

RESILIENCE IS A CONTINUOUS PROCESS

Based on clinical experience and studies, a resilient person has the ability to move towards the tools that they need to cope with challenging circumstances and can manage to access these tools in a positive way. Resilience is a complex and fluidly process and never a static state. The fact is, even some personal attributes that we frequently associate with resilience are most often triggered by our surroundings, be they biological or cognitive. Resilience, therefore, means that your world will provide you with tools that are useful to you. It is therefore safe to conclude that resilience is not just on the inside.

IT'S EASIER TO CHANGE THING AROUND YOU THAN CONTINUOUSLY CHANGING YOURSELF

Suppose you are really tired of work and under great pressure. Do you get up at 5 am every day and try to focus on meditation and yoga? At the same time, at work, you will still encounter toxic bosses and employees who bully you. Is this really the right effort? Or is it better to find opportunities to change the environment? For example, by finding a different department in the business section to work in thus automatically escapes the person who bullied you, or changing your working hours? Even this requires a certain personal motivation, but it does not change you, rather it changes the world around you. Let us take another example, assuming you feel alone at work what do you do? What about being the individual on the team who knows everyone's birthdays and brings the cake and encourages everyone to be more accommodating or social?

RESILIENCE REQUIRES FACING PROBLEMS WITH THE INTENTION TO SOLVE THEM

Collect information. Think creatively of a variety of ways to do it that can get you closer to a solution. Look for a lot of possibilities. If they do not solve the problem, gather more information and consider additional options. In the meantime, doing something positive to get what you want will fuel your desire to keep coming back from frustration and disappointment. A problem-solving approach to life's problems provides one of the ultimate path to resilience.

PATHWAYS TO RESILENCE

Resilience is a great ability that lets you easily heal from difficulties. When you're tough, you come up when life takes you down, and you keep going. Most of the times even the battles of life will make you more grounded and turn you into a stronger individual. Here are what I perceived as pathways to resilience.

1. STOP THE NEGATIVE THINKING CYCLES

And when bad things happen, we're left worrying about negative consequences. We're continually discussing what we ought to have improved previously that we fail to do. We're ruminating over these things, and tempted to reason that talking over our issues again and again will assist us in conquering them. Unfortunately, such reasoning will have us enveloped by our feelings and disturb us from, making the necessary strides to push ahead.

To stop these negative thinking cycles, you can get involve in any thing that involve your body and your mind as a means of intentional distracting your thinking pattern. Such things include deep breathing over a period of time, exercises and dancing to music.

2. **STOP THE "CATASTROPHIZING"**

Catastrophizing is when we foresee the worst possible result of a scenario. For instance, you might have lost your work, so now you're beginning to feel that you're never going to make it, and that everybody's going to think that you're a failure forever. This could sound too extreme because most of us don't catastrophize that much, but plenty of us still imagine that the worst possible scenarios will come true. While monitoring conceivable negative results might be useful in planning ahead, when we accept that the worst will occur, we set ourselves up for pointless pressure and weak resilience.

One approach to break this example of thought is to wear a pendant or hold a stone or a little item with you always. Each time you end up imaging the most noticeably awful scene — an individual, a circumstance, or a result — you go and touch the item. When handling the item, remind yourself that the best possible outcome is as likely to occur just as the worst possible outcome. However, it doesn't make you any happier to think about.

By controlling our negative thoughts, they are no longer so scary. We began to see negative thoughts come and go, and we have the ability to deal with them. Now, we can begin to actively respond to challenges that give us the opportunity to develop resilience and improve our lives in unpredictable and surprising ways.

3. **OVERCOME THAT FEAR OF FAILURE**

Most of us are scared of failure; we are worried that if we fail, people will think poorly of us, and we feel humiliated when we fail. But by treating failure as a disease or an enemy that need to be avoided, we never give ourselves a chance to overcome challenges and practice resilience. As a result, we are stopping ourselves from being more adaptive. And how are you going to overcome the fear of disappointment and that you can continue creating resilience?

When you believe failure defeat is a threat, like many of us do, your body will brace for a fight — and you will feel like you're in a war. On the other hand, if you see something hard, something you might struggle to do, as a surmountable obstacle, then you're more inclined to believe you 're capable of doing it. As a bonus, when you see obstacles that you might have to face as challenges, you 're actually going to be more competent and less likely to fail.

To establish this "challenging way of thinking", please reflect on the challenges you have overcome in the past. Suppose you are worried about starting a new job. Take a moment to recall the other goals you have achieved. Remind yourself that you have succeeded in the past, even though in smaller things. When you remind yourself that you have been successful before, your mind will be shifted toward a "challenge mind-set"

Next, visualize success. By imagining yourself doing well, you will change your mind-set to do well. On the other hand, if you reflect on where the problem might be, your fear will increase, and you are now more likely to experience what you are afraid of. Remember, even if you can move your brain to stop seeing something as a threat, you may still feel nervous or anxious, but you will also experience positive physiological changes that can help you make better use of these negative emotions.

4. **FIND BENEFITS FROM PAST PROBLEMS AND FAILURES**

Many smart people will tell you that once you encounter failure, you should reflect on your failure. But negative emotions can obscure your thinking. If you are still hurt by your experience with failure however, it may be not be practicable to take note of the gains of your bitter experience. If you are not familiar with this approach, then the easier way to find the benefits of failure may be to look at past failures, which no longer bother you. By practising to discover the benefits of past challenges, you can enhance this feature to easily discover benefits next time.

In order to find benefits, first list what you have learned from past failures. For example, if you missed an significant deadline, you might learn that you must henceforth need to focus more, delegate more, or reduce your flair for perfectionism. Seek to find as many benefits as you can think of. Ask yourself these questions to help you.

- Are there, or would there be, any good consequences arising from this situation?
- Are you thankful for some aspect of the situation?
- What are you better off than when you started?
- What did you learn to do?
- How did you mature, change and develop as a result of this situation?

5. **EMOTIONALLY DETACH YOURSELF TO OBSTACLES**

If you face a dilemma, the desire to talk about your feelings as though you were "a fly on the wall," or as if you were someone else who is experiencing your feelings from a distance, stops you from being lost with your negative emotions. With emotional distancing you won't feel as guilty as you felt when the incident happened.

Second, to learn this strategy, recall the recent traumatic confrontation you have had with another human. Make sure to pick one that is really specific. Recall, for example, that "You got into a fight with John to miss your birthday." Try not to talk about the fight with John in general.

Now re-imagine the incident from the point of view of an outside observer — for example, from the point of view of a stranger on the street.

Ask yourself the following questions to practice being a stranger:

- Would the listener be able to comprehend why you're angry?
- Will the strange outsider be able to see the point of view of the other person?
- How would the observer assess the situation?
- Could this outsider see the situation differently than you?

Trying being an outside observer helps make the experience looks less intense.

6. **KNOW, IT WILL SURELY PASS**

Another technique that can help you better deal with stress involves thinking about the outcomes of stressful events in the relatively distant future. For example, you might say, "Time will heal all the wounds," or "This, too, is going to pass."

The ability to think about a future where you will no longer feel so bad about anything you're struggling with, helps you get through difficult experiences. It may reduce the severity of the negative emotions and the discomfort caused by the incident. So next time you 're in the midst of stressful situations, try looking back at the situation standing in the future.

7. FIND THE SILVER LININGS

The capability to see silver linings in negative or challenging circumstances allows us to generate optimistic feelings, even when all seems hopeless. Searching for silver linings can help alleviate negative feelings, relieve fatigue, and speed up recovery from traumatic incidents.

The next time you encounter a challenging situation that tends to leave you downcast,use your creativity and secure anything that would make you feel better about the experience.

8. REAPPRAISAL PRACTICE WHILE WATCHING MOVIES

If you're having a hard time seeing silver linings in your own life, it may be better to do that in other people's lives. To use the experience of others to practice reassessment, plan to practice the next time you want to watch a film.

Looking at the scene or the video, think about what might be gained from the encounter, or consider potential successful results. Keeping these thoughts in mind, think about what tips you can give the characters about how to feel better. Now, ask yourself, how do I apply this advice to my own life the next time I feel sad, anxious, or angry?

9. FIND THE ADVANTAGES OF LIFE

Benefit analysis is similar to reassessment, which can be found in negative, neutral or positive conditions. You may argue, for example, that the advantages of working in a very tough position are that you learn new skills and develop character.

Yet you could also argue that the advantages of a very easy career are that you feel comfortable and have more time to commit to those things you love. With some practice, you can find the benefits of any situation.

To practice seeking rewards, first talk of a potentially bad experience you've had recently. Seek not to choose an experience that is incredibly negative — it's important to choose an experience that isn't too bad when you first wan learn how to use this technique. You can work through tougher experiences as you become more skilled. For example, maybe your car broke down or you got into a small fight with a friend of yours.

Now it's time for you to try. It's all right. Start by spending a couple of minutes talking about the implications of a bad experience. Consider asking for as many opportunities as you can think about. Ask yourself the brainstorm questions.

- Are there, or would there be, any good consequences arising from this situation?
- Why are you better off now than before you started?

10. USING YOUR NEGATIVE FEELINGS TO PUSH YOURSELF

Negative feelings like sorrow and depression tend to express to us that we need their love and compassion. Bad feelings like anger will help inspire us to take action, change our lives, and maybe change the world. At their heart, feelings are built to direct our actions in essential ways. Casually putting aside negative emotions without reflecting on where they come from can leave us stuck and unable to move forward in the way we want.

And when life throws you into a ditch and you feel bad, ask yourself, "Is this pessimistic feeling trying to tell me something? "Can you move the negative emotion away from leaving this negative emotion untouched? Is there anything that needs to be done to protect this negative sentiment from arising again in the future? If so, don't drive it away — use it to fuel change in your life or in the world.

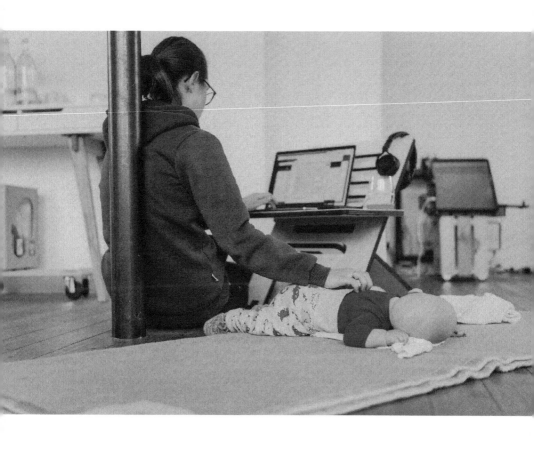

YOUR WORK AND FAMILY

Mompreneurs always have difficult times. They are occupied with the impossible job of being completely dedicated to work and home. As an employee or a mother, it may be frustrating and thankless, being viewed as not completely present. But it doesn't need to be like this.

If you learn to find a balance that works for your life, it is possible to follow a rewarding full-time career while taking an active role as a mother.

The following tips will help busy moms to make it a little easier to juggle the two sides.

1. **Stop feeling guilty**

   Mothers are too often judged after returning to work full time for "abandoning their children, while fathers are forced to go to work to provide for the family. In our seemingly modern culture, why is this sexist stereotype still so present?

Some women have no choice but to be a stay-at-home wife, and others want to go back to work because they don't want to give up their job. Whatever the cause, it is a decision that should be respected, not punished or shamed, to opt to be a working mom. It's time to let it go if you're feeling bad for not being with your kid all the time.

Focus on the good aspects that contribute to your families in your work life. Be assured that for your entire family, including yourself, you are making the right decision and your child will know the depth of your affection and appreciate your sacrifice.

2. **Use time saving hacks**

Use shortcuts and schedule carefully to get the most done with the shortest period of time.

Order your food online and use the curbside pick-up or get it shipped to your house; this saves time and means that nothing is forgotten.

During your commute, arrange phone calls and get short orders completed in your lunch hour to clear up more time in the week.

Plan the clothes to wear and your lunch the night before, so that instead of hurrying to get out the door on time, you can enjoy your morning.

3. Find childcare providers that you trust

Realizing that your kid is cared for is key to getting peace of mind while you're at work. Find your child's daycare, nanny, or someone you know you should trust.

Flexible hours, a low teacher-to-child ratio, a safe and spacious atmosphere and up-to-date permits should be available for quality daycare.

Look for one with comprehensive experience and excellent credentials for nannies. If it's a good match, have at least one trial day to observe and make all the objectives plain from the get-go. Keep in regular touch during the day if possible and request for photos and pictures of your little one.

4. **Avoid distractions and time wasting**

When you are a working mother, time is such a scarce luxury. At work, be mindful of the time you spend socializing with co-workers if your productivity is impaired. Limit long lunch breaks and internet surfing so that you can make the best of your time at work.

Be concerned and connected to your hubby and your child while at home, rather than your phone or TV, to make sure that the time spent together is positive and deliberate.

5. **Connect with other working moms**

It's not only you. There are millions of working moms on a regular basis who are going through that same thing you are battling with.

During the week, full-time mothers have more freedom to schedule meet-ups, but working moms should have the same kind of group as well.

Check for co-workers who are working mothers as well on a totally different basis, these are people you would be able to talk to. On the weekends or take walks together at college, arrange play-dates and mom parties. Using Facebook communities, Meet-up, and some applications to locate working moms near you.

It will remind you that you don't have to do this all alone by laughing together, telling stories, and discovering your friends.

6. **Reconnect with your partner**

The secret to a happier family is a happy marriage. Give your marriage a priority and it would have a huge effect on everything else.

If necessary, locate a childcare to put your kid and go out for a normal date night. Do the stuff you both loved doing before you became parents. Plan something else besides dinner at your usual location, like a drawing lesson or a quiz party. Have an open talk with your partner that doesn't include work or kids, and listen to what he has to say.

7. **Create special and meaningful family activities**

Let the time you spend with your family always count by organizing event that everyone will appreciate and be excited with.

Plan a weekly family game day, hold a picnic in the garden, or play mini golf. I enjoy doing long walks with my family in the local parks, because it offers us an opportunity to be active and have interesting conversations. Press the older children for suggestions and let them get interested in choosing where to travel.

8. **Stay organized by planning ahead using calendars and lists.**

The emotional load that must be taken on by working mothers is a task that nobody else can understand. You are responsible for keeping track of medical visits, signing slips of approval, taking potluck plates, acknowledging birthdays, writing cards, being on top of clothing and sizes, knowing what's in the refrigerator and pantry, never making the house run out of toilet paper, just to name a few.

Using calendars, apps, and other tools to maintain track with your never-ending to-do and let some of your mental weight go. With me, I'm attaching activities to a shared calendar so that my husband can quickly see what's going on and help out. I still use Google Keep as a place to create lists and take notes so it's simple to exchange capabilities. Plan ahead and get ready as much as possible, so that little is left for last minute run around.

9. **Share the housework**

The housework responsibility does not be entirely on the shoulders of a woman. This is an environment in which your partner can easily support you out, especially if you have complex activities that only you can do (i.e. breastfeeding, putting the baby down).

Delegate basic tasks to them if the children are older, so that they can learn to develop healthy habits early on and take an active part in contributing to the family.

Spending money on a cleaning service is another thing to explore. It can be hard to justify wasting money on things that you can do yourself, but if it is a big cause of tension to have an unkempt home, it will be very well spent money.

10. **Say yes to less**

If it is giving you more discomfort than fun, you don't have to say yes to every single party invitation or extracurricular activity.

Determine how much your calendar can accommodate and pick the most fun events for your boy. Don't feel guilty saying no to the lot of them. Overbooking sucks all the fun out of the experience and leaves little time for the downtime that is desperately needed.

11. **Lower your expectations**

Expecting that moms have to prepare nutritious and tasty meals every day, keep a completely clean home, and be the ideal parent are the pressures that you place on yourself. No one else is asking as much as you expect of yourself.

If you lower your expectations, you can notice that a lot of needless tension can be avoided.

Your house doesn't need to be spotless any time a visitor comes over, particularly if the guest has children as well.

Buying cookies instead of making them on your own would not make you a horrible mother. Home-cooked meals every day is a wonderful aim, but occasionally eating out as a family doesn't mean you're wasteful!

12. **Make time for "me time"**

In the hectic world of work and home life, finding time for yourself is key in maintaining inner harmony and order.

Find the time and an exercise regularly .It will encourage you to relax and be refreshed. Other things to create time for include, meditation, reading, blogging, catching up with a friend, or pampering yourself. For me, writing in my appreciation journal is one thing I want to do during "me time". This encourages me to understand issues better, put things in context and make my fears and anxieties feel less important.

MOMPRENEURS AND SEX

In a previous chapter I spoke about the need to have sex regularly with your hubby. Without the fear of placing too much emphasis, let me state categorically that this is a very important subject if you want to succeed at home and at work. Here are the major reasons why I believe you need regular sex as a working mother!

1. You look younger

   At a psychology conference, Dr. David Weeks, a clinical neuropsychologist at the Royal Edinburgh Hospital, revealed that his detailed research showed that older men and women involved in sex were 5 to 7 years younger than their actual age.

   But every night, you don't have to be there to experience the results of enhanced youth! In fact, Weeks discovered in his 10-year research that quality is as important as quantity.

2. It boosts your fertility as a couple

   It has been observed that repeated intercourse can control the hormones of a woman and controls her cycles, which may further improve the likelihood of conceiving.

   For men, studies also found that the more you make love, the higher the consistency of your sperm will be. This will sound like music to most men's ears.

   The wellbeing of semen was determined to be highest when sex had last happened less than two days before the sperm was examined and after 10 days of abstinence it was substantially diminished.

   If you are looking for a child as a working mum you are advised to cooperate with your hubby for regular sex so as to keep the sperm new and in tip-top condition and not just around the time of your ovulation.

3. It helps to fight colds and flu

   It has been found that having sex once or twice a week raises the levels of an antibody called immunoglobulin A or IgA in your body that will shield you from colds and flu. One research showed that those who have sex more than once a week have IgA levels that are 30 percent higher than those who abstain.

4. Disease-proof your body

   It is assumed that possessing elevated levels of the natural steroid DHEA, known as the "anti-aging hormone," is essential to maintaining the body fitter for longer. DHEA is secreted in the body during intercourse, and the volume in the bloodstream soars to five times the usual amount following an orgasm.

5. Lengthen your life

    A research undertaken in Australia showed that individuals who reached sexual peak at least three times a week had a fifty per cent lower risk of dying for some medical cause than someone who just climaxed once a month.

    An 80-year research conducted by Stanford University psychology called the Longevity Experiment studied women who regularly orgasmed. The researchers then revisited the women to see how long they existed, and the findings found overwhelmingly that women who lived longer than their counterparts who did so less often had a higher likelihood of reaching orgasm during sex.

6. **Shift your middle-age spread and keep fit**

    Thirty minutes of active sex burns up to 100 calories, the same as a tiny bottle of wine. And if you have relatively involved sex twice a week, you burn an additional 5,000 calories a year! varying your roles is also a great, enjoyable way to tone out various muscle groups and maintain your limbs lean and healthy.

7. Ease menstruation cramps

    Some women claim their menstrual discomfort reduces if they perform the deed after a cramp strike.

    One hypothesis is that muscular contractions that arise as you hit peak stages of arousal alleviate stress in the muscles of your uterus – those that induce menstrual cramps – and ease the discomfort.

8. Helps minimize the incidence of incontinence

    Healthy sex is a perfect exercise for a woman's pelvic floor muscles – muscles that regulate orgasms – it even stems the release of semen, eliminating discharge and incontinence.

    Pregnancy and your chance of developing stress incontinence and prolapse later.

    And let's face it, sex is much more fun than doing pelvic floor workouts on your own!

    Menopause can substantially weaken these muscles, but the stronger they are the lower

9. It can prevent a heart attack

    Many studies have shown that regular sex can deter, not bring about, heart problems, as once feared. One research at Queen's University Belfast showed that the chance of heart disease or stroke may be halved by having sex three days a week.

    Another research in Israel showed that people who experienced two orgasms a week were up to 30% less likely than those who did not like intercourse or had an orgasm to have heart disease.

10. Increase your attractiveness to others

    High sexual activity allows more pheromones to be emitted by the body, chemicals that increase the attraction to the opposite sex.

    Therefore the more sex you had with your partner, the greater your urge to have sex with them again would be.

11. Smooth out your wrinkles

    The hormone oestrogen is spilled out during sex, which can have a plumping effect on the face in turn helping to smooth out those fine lines. This is especially helpful during menopause, since as the levels of oestrogen spontaneously decline, a woman's skin can become drier and more wrinkled.

    One American analysis found that menopausal women who had sex per week had estrogen levels that were twice as high as their colleagues who abstained.

12. It offers you a healthy glow

    Sex encourages skin renewal, since it is an aerobic type of exercise, according to studies carried out at the Royal Edinburgh Hospital.

    The scientist behind this research discovered that vigorous sex pumps higher oxygen levels across the body, improves blood and nutrient supply to the skin, and pushes healthy, fresher skin cells to the surface, making the skin appear healthier.

13. Enhance your self-esteem

    In a new study commissioned by the University of Texas, US, one of the most notable advantages was that people who had intercourse frequently were more positive about their bodies.

14. Lower your blood pressure

    Men and women who had enough of sex coped better with tension and had lower blood pressure than people who abstained, a Scottish research showed. Researchers at the U.S. University of Brigham Young have associated regular intercourse with lower systolic blood pressure.

15. Banish depression

Sex stimulates the brain to produce feel-good hormones that improve your serotonin levels, the positive hormone, to boost your mood, like any activity that increases the heart rate.

Serotonin is the primary antidepressant chemical in the body and one of the biggest explanations why after sex people smile and feel satisfied and comfortable.

According to a survey of about 300 people by psychologist Gordon Gallup in the American Archives Of Sexual Activity, sexually engaged women in long-term marriages are often less prone to be insecure than women who go without intercourse.

16. Cure that headache

Catching a headache" may be an age-old excuse for not having sex, but the empirical proof says that sex can help shift pain on the contrary!"

This is because love-making triggers a rise in the oxytocin "love" hormone, and other feel-good endorphins, which may relieve suffering. Women also recorded post-coitus changes in their suffering from both headaches and arthritis.

Lessens Pain

Try to get an orgasm before you reach for the aspirin.

Barry R. Komisaruk, PhD, a distinguished service professor at Rutgers, New Jersey State University, says: "Orgasm can block pain." It activates a hormone that helps increase the threshold for pain.

Stimulation without orgasm can do the trick as well. We have observed that vaginal stimulation can block chronic pain in the back and leg, and we have been advised by many women that genital self-stimulation can alleviate menstrual cramps, arthritic pain, and even headache in some cases," says Komisaruk."

17. Slash stress

Researchers observed in a report in the Psychology Journal that people who had sex in the last 24 hours coped with unpleasant situations, such as public speaking, differently than someone who had not.

Study has also shown that before and after sex, touching and cuddling lowers the levels of cortisol in the body, the hormone that is emitted when you are nervous.

18. Kick away insomnia .

Having sex makes you sleep easier, something that we can both use. Your body secretes the hormone oxytocin, also called the 'heart hormone,' when you bond with your husband. That's actually the same hormone responsible for bonding with your infant, particularly while breastfeeding. Just before climax, both males and females emit this feel-good hormone, and it encourages comfort and sleepiness as it flows through the brain. And with more sleep, a brighter morning arrives before running off to work and kicking a serious ass in the office, juggling a lot of kids. So say yes,when your significant other tries to get frisky next time.

19. **Strengthen your bones**

Since natural sex in postmenopausal women may increase oestrogen levels, it may provide some protection against bone-thinning osteoporosis due to oestrogen deficiency.

And men can also benefit, since testosterone levels have been shown to increase during and after sex, which can provide some protection against male osteoporosis.

20. **Cut your risk of prostate cancer**

Researchers at Nottingham University have found that for men who enjoy a daily sex life in their 50s, there is a decreased risk of developing prostate cancer.

This is how sex clears the prostate of toxins that would otherwise accumulate cancerous changes and cause them.

The correlation was first indicated after several studies discovered that monks appeared to have a higher chance of developing prostate cancer.

You'll Be Happier

Intimate couples are healthier. A 2016 University of Toronto Mississauga study showed that couples who had sex even once a week were more happy, and it was almost as important as more sex to sustain an emotional relationship with your partner during the week.

Ultimately, if the parents are happy, the children are happy. If everybody is satisfied, odds are you're off on the right foot every day in your career.

21. Feel better all day

If you plan to go for a spot of morning love to start the day,- according to research-you can keep up with your mood right into the night.

The American scientist Dr. Debby Herbenick discovered that adults who first made love in the morning were not only more upbeat for the remainder of the day but also gained from a better immune system than those who merely opted for a cup of tea and some toast before leaving the house.

22. You'll Have a Better Memory

According to a number of recent studies—including a 2016 study published by the Oxford University Press, frequent sex is linked to a healthier brain. The original study found not only generating new neurons, but also enhanced cognitive function. They found that women who have more sex are more likely to remember more complex words. As if your verbal skills weren't already off-the-charts, now with a bit more bedroom play, you're apt to use that killer memory of yours to tell your teenager what's what with more wit and sarcasm than even her 13 year-old brain can muster. Or, to nail the meeting with your new client, showing off how much you learned about their business using your superior vocabulary.

You'll Be More Productive

According to a 2017 Oregon State report released in the Journal of Administration, sex improves your efficiency the next day. The more creative and energized you feel after a vigorous bedroom romp, the more likely you are to kill your child's school Valentine's Day party by producing your next power point presentation or creating DIY crafts. It's also known to improve work satisfaction. To feel sexually wanted and needed is empowering.

Gender improves efficiency and managers should be delighted to realize this! So, managers, tell the staff to get home with their partners and get comfortable. That would make for a fascinating memo from the workplace.

Use these next 2 pages to write down some changes you promise to make.

HOME ORGANIZATION
FOR MOMPRENEURS

Home organizing is not simple, particularly when you're working outside your home. Piles of dirty linen, hungry teenagers, school assignments and dinner waiting to be made don't permit a happy return to homely comfort after a wearying day in the workplace. So what would you be doing to optimize your everyday schedule and virtually every part of your life?

You're still working as a mom. There are individuals who look up to you and want you to deliver; meanwhile your 4-year-old is at home waiting for mom to help out with the assignment from the school. Work gets much more challenging when you have a full-time job that occupies 40 hours a week.

Each working mother faces her own series of special difficulties and circumstances. You're going to have to figure out a solution that ideally fits you and lets you handle your home and your job easier.

Here are few ideas about how to tame the time management beast in your own special way, concentrating on staying organized at in the house.

WHAT'S THE TOUGHEST ORDEAL?

It is crucial that you evaluate your activities and recognize those that overwhelm you most. If you've figured out a strategy to minimize them, you'll find your life clear from most of your clutter. Certainly, these stress-causing tasks differ from one working mother to another.

SETTING THE DINNER DEBACLE CORRECTLY

When you are scared of having to cook food after a long day, try basic time-tested tricks such as menu planning. Plan your menus for next week and finish your weekend shopping. When you come back from the office tired and starving, this will spare you a lot of stress and confusion.

Other advantages to menu planning include reduced intake of frozen and unhealthy junk food, more balanced home-made food, and fewer money on going out for lunch. You could also cut down on excessive grocery purchases in the middle of the week.

Menu planning calls for some evening cooking. If you need to assist your children with homework or whether there are other social responsibilities in the evening that makes it challenging to spare time, a Slow-Cooker Recipes is the perfect option.

Preparing in advance will make the meal enjoyable and enjoyable. Prepare all supplies the night before. Cut the beef, chop the onion, weigh the seasoning, and prepare the food. Put them in the refrigerator, in the early morning, all you have to do is put them in a bowl, then turn on the slow cooker and enjoy a delicious home-cooked dinner in the evening.

GETTING CHILDREN SET IN THE MORNING

Jumping out of bed, getting ready, grabbing a cup of coffee and being off to work on time is not easy. When you have a crying 5-year-old to wake up, feed and dress, pack lunch and drop off for kindergarten, the job becomes more challenging. So, prepare and deal smartly with weekday mornings.

With lost homework sheets, folders, keys and misplaced backpacks, do not add to the madness of the mornings. Have all together the night before.

Help your child pack his backpack so that in the morning he's ready to go. Box lunches and get them refrigerated. Get your satchel ready for work so you don't lose any vital files or paperwork.

Lay out the clothing, both for yourself and your boy, for the next day. It's better if you can prepare clothes for a week for your kid and place them on hangers for each day of the week with a color-coded mark.

Make sure that you wake up before your kids for at least an hour. This will give you enough time for the family to get dressed, have your coffee in the morning and have breakfast ready. You should concentrate on getting them dressed and off to school once the children are awake.

HOUSEHOLD DUTIES ARE MANAGEABLE

It's best to set aside the fantasies of achieving an immaculate and spotlessly clean house once you've had kids at least until your children go off to college.

If you are into have a full-time job, it's going to be challenging to find the time needed to clean up and fix the whole house with a single super cleaning session. You're going to have to handle one space or job at a time.

Dealing with the clumsy issue is going to make your house breathe free and fast. Quite definitely, rather than dirt or dusts, it's the mountains of items thrown here and there that make your house look messy

Get the support of available people to keep the house tidy. Let your children participate in the cleaning. Little kids enjoy lending a helpful hand and taking responsibilities. You should distribute duties appropriately and remind your kids to water the flowers, keep the toys, and lay the bed. You should even tutor them to put everything in their rightful place and cleans their plates and cutleries personally after dinner.

Hiring skilled cleaners can bring a lot of relief to an overworked mother. If possible, plan for a cheap cleaning aid every month. Such an arrangement can save you a lot of hassle and also allow you make time for more crucial issues, such as a visit to your dentist or a major meeting with your bank officer

DON'T SNUFF OUT ROMANCE

Label the day in the planner for a date night. Plan well in ahead to have babysitting appointments so you can both spend the night out with each other. If necessary, go on a little vacation with your spouse as your kids have fun at the summer camp. Do not let the pressure of regular activity wipe out the joy of your marriage.

MAKE ROOM FOR FRIENDS AND HAVE SOME FUN

The days of carefree girlhood are far behind you, but that shouldn't deter you from spending a night out with your girlfriends. This is a special luxury for working mothers, so make sure you appreciate me whenever you can. Get your hubby to sit at home whilst shopping with your buddies or catch up with the latest news at a neighborhood café. Friends take the pressure out of your stressed life and offer you a shoulder to rest on so cherish and cultivate those ties.

In conclusion, a working mother places everything and everybody ahead of herself. It's crucial that you really pay attention and take care of yourself. Work to suit your schedule but be flexible. Be dynamic, go with the flow and be settled .If things do not work out as planned, let it go, relax, tomorrow is another day

Conclusion

Y ou can be a wife, a mother, and an entrepreneur. Some have done it with the society's support, and some have struggled against countless odds to prove the same. It is both attractive and productive for mothers to work in today's society, just as their husbands too. In the developed world, even in the throes of a male-oriented society and tradition, we should understand that a working woman can potentially be a great mother, counter to conventional assumptions that a working mother can never be a responsible mom.

A working mother can manage her home and work effectively and enjoy the excitement offered by a job or profession. In order to make an impact, she not only feels better for herself, but is also compelled to take better care of herself. A good career, along with motherhood, adds to the completeness of being a woman. However, owing to alleged negligence of the parental role, the major pressures of becoming a working mother remain: lack of time and a sense of guilt. There are however many benefits, including personal comfort, fulfilled vision, financial rewards and enriched family life.

Significant changes as discussed in this book are required at personal level and at the workplace to reap all the rewards of "mompreneurship", allowing the woman to fulfil the dual obligations of career and motherhood.

The working mother is the epitome of modern womanhood. The new workplace climate has to take into consideration the unique needs of this working populace, moving its orientation from male domination to gender neutrality and parenting friendly policies. Both the extended and the nuclear family members need to respond appropriately to the demands of the working mother in order to enable a healthier family growth

If you would like to learn more about my business endeavors or how you can
start making Passive income so that you can spend more time with your family. Please visit my website www.Hood2Heights.com

You can also follow me on my social media Pages:

Facebook.com/Hood2Heights
Instagram.com/Hood2Heights

Made in the USA
Columbia, SC
12 February 2021

32853269R00089